THE POWER OF
SHAKTI

"An excellent sourcebook for both women and men, every page of The
Power of Shakti *provides new insight into the rich, vibrant energy of
the Divine Feminine. It offers a profound pathway to understanding
the power and potency of this essential feminine current as it flows
through the sacred temple of the physical body, linking us to the
Galactic Center. In these shifting times of planetary transformation,
this book assists us in rediscovering our intimate connection to nature,
the earth, and the cosmos."*

SHARRON ROSE, AUTHOR OF *THE PATH OF THE PRIESTESS* AND
FILM PRODUCER OF *2012 THE ODYSSEY* AND *TIMEWAVE 2013*

*"*The Power of Shakti *is revolutionary and is bound to open the gates
that have kept us from our true power as both men and women. It taps
in to the heart of the ancient mysteries and articulates their modern-
day message to we humans. Reading this material or attending Padma
Prakasha's seminars will rock your world."*

LINDA STAR WOLF, AUTHOR OF *SHAMANIC BREATHWORK*
AND COAUTHOR OF *SHAMANIC MYSTERIES OF EGYPT: AWAKENING
THE HEALING POWER OF THE HEART*

"The Power of Shakti *will revitalize your life by revealing the patterns of energy that flow between the physical body and the galactic universe. Equally esoteric and practical, it offers illuminating insight into holistic health through scholarly understanding of the body's dynamic light field. The author's profound integrity, knowledge, and experience enrich every page. This is not an ordinary book; it is unique, provocative, and fresh.*"

ISHA LERNER, AUTHOR OF *THE TRIPLE GODDESS TAROT* AND *INNER CHILD CARDS*

THE POWER OF
SHAKTI

18 Pathways to Ignite
the Energy of the Divine Woman

PADMA AON PRAKASHA

Destiny Books
Rochester, Vermont • Toronto, Canada

Destiny Books
One Park Street
Rochester, Vermont 05767
www.DestinyBooks.com

Destiny Books is a division of Inner Traditions International

Library of Congress Cataloging-in-Publication Data
Prakasha, Padma Aon.
  The power of Shakti : 18 pathways to ignite the energy of the divine woman / Padma Aon Prakasha.
     p. cm.
  Includes index.
  ISBN 978-1-59477-316-7 (pbk.)
  1. Sex—Religious aspects—Tantrism. 2. Sakti (Hindu deity) I. Title.
  HQ64.P73 2009
  306.77082—dc22

                                                                    2009022782

Printed and bound in the United States

10   9   8   7   6

Illustrations by Amaya Dubois
Text design and layout by Virginia Scott Bowman
This book was typeset in Garamond Premiere Pro with Aries and Myriad Pro as display typefaces

Any correspondence for the author can be sent to his website: **www.padmaaon.com**

Contents

cᴈ⋙ᴂↄ

PART ONE
Pathways to the Womb

∾

PART THREE
Shakti Awakened

A Note to the Reader on the Writing of This Book

IN ONE SENSE THIS IS a unique and co-creative book written by Shakti through many people in her flow. Several people who have worked with the Shakti Circuit practices have recounted their experiences in their own words—or in the words of Shakti speaking through them. Where possible, these people have been quoted directly in the text and have been acknowledged by their initials at the end of their quotations. The experiences and voices of others have been incorporated into the text as part of the flow of wisdom. The contribution of these participants is part of the one womb that is created when we come together in the Shakti Circuit.

Preface

IN HINDUISM, SHAKTI IS THE creative power of life-force energy—the flow that connects your body, mind, and soul. The Shakti Circuit is a way of establishing an ideal flow of this life-force energy via eighteen pathways that we can access in our bodies.

The Shakti Circuit is based on multiple forms of Tantra yoga found in the Indian, Tibetan, and Hebrew sacred traditions. These forms of Tantra were originally part of the one teaching or original Tantra practiced thousands of years ago, before they were separated piece by piece into different traditions to preserve their sanctity and the transformative power that they hold.

Tantra in this sense is the science of weaving all the aspects of your self into a unified tapestry, circulating sound, light, breath, and loving sexual power throughout the universe of your bodymind and soul. This is achieved through the medium of the Shakti Circuit, a technology held within us that connects and unifies our bodymind and soul with all of creation. The purpose of practicing the Shakti Circuit is to reveal the living experience within yourself of loving wisdom and blissful power: primordial creative unity.

I have been Initiated over the last thirteen years to bring the pieces of the eighteen pathways of the Shakti Circuit back together again. My journey has taken me to over sixty countries, to hundreds of sacred sites known and unknown, and to various teachers, most of whom are not known, some of whom don't even have a name, and all of whom have no wish to be known in the world at large. It has been my role to be Initiated into multiple lineages, to meditate in Samadhi to receive the wisdom of these lineages, and then to share it in a form that is accessible and understandable for you today.

Lineage transmissions are not linear. After an authentic Initiation one's life changes drastically, and one can receive, through the four stages of the science of sound, all the wisdom the lineage has accumulated over thousands of years. This transmission is authorized by the elders of a given tradition, many of whom may have passed on from their bodies into the spirit world.

Being an initiate of multiple sacred traditions allows one to experience the interconnections of all traditions, rather than just see it from an intellectual perspective. In India, the ability to learn is known as *smriti* and *sruti:* learning through tradition, and receiving wisdom through revelation after certain aspects of the tradition have been mastered.

Once an Initiate is clear and beginning to teach the tradition, the mainstay of his or her material comes through authentic revelation in meditation. This is the basis of the Awakened sacred traditions. The more one teaches, the more the lineage gives to be shared. This is especially true today, as all the mystical traditions are opening doors to their secrets in order to accelerate transformation in those who genuinely desire it, and who are committed to doing the deep inner work required to accomplish this noble goal.

This book is experiential: it is based on real transformative experiences that people have each time they delve into the Shakti Circuit. Each pathway works, and together they create the experience of *spanda*—the whole bodymind and soul vibrating in complete resonance with the wave of life. This is perhaps the simplest, yet most transformative experience we can have of the nature of life itself.

I have used few esoteric terms or spiritual jargon in this book. What is needed now is the return of the power of Woman, as simple as it is profound, and this is the reason this book and teachings on the eighteen pathways are being shared, taught, and released again on Earth.

I have used the word *womb* many times, and have sometimes included the word *hara* for men. Men, please do not feel left out: I have seen many a man who begins to refer to his hara as his womb, and is transformed in the process. If we choose to harness the tremendous power of the womb we can use it to birth ourselves regardless of gender.

The eighteen pathways of the Shakti Circuit are nothing new. They are ancient yet timeless, and apply to all human beings, regardless of caste, color, race, or religion. They have been practiced before and are held in many lineages, and thus have support from many lineages in their resurfacing again in the world. They are universal in nature, as they go to the core of creation and the human experience: Shakti, the feminine flow of life force, free, wild, without border or boundary, free of concept, ideation, and ideal. Simple and unique to each person, Shakti can free you of need by allowing you to give. This is perhaps the greatest gift of all.

Introduction

SHAKTI IS THE LIVING POWER of the Goddess, the creative force that manifests. It is the complement of Shiva, pure consciousness that does not create or manifest. Shakti is the energy that puts into action the higher "thoughts" of Shiva, for Shiva cannot create without Shakti. Shakti does not know what to manifest without the principles of Shiva guiding her. These principles of yin and yang are constantly working within us, and need each other in order for us to be in balance and harmony.

Shiva without Shakti is ideas without passion, thought without the ability to manifest or flow. Shakti without Shiva is life force with no direction or form to go into: chaos. In the living dance between the two, we (and our world) are created. In recent times, the power of Shakti has been forgotten as more masculine ideas and structures have taken precedence.

In India, Shakti is the wife of Shiva. Known by many names such as Kali, Parvati, and Durga, Shakti is worshipped by hundreds of millions of people, and for many of them she has more importance than Shiva. Her grace and ability to manifest anything draws people to her, as does her willingness to love and care for the human side of life. She is very much on Earth as an embodied Presence; she does not leave the creation nor is she seen as transcendent, separate from nature, or up in heaven somewhere. She is right here, in us, now.

Shakti is the essence of sexuality, which manifests and creates both form and life. She is also the passion for life and the engagement with life. As the creative force that births and regenerates, Shakti connects each of us to our essence, even as she weaves her way through the web of life and connects us all.

Shakti is sensual, rich, and overflowing. She is the Mother, Lover, Creator, and Destroyer. She manifests in order to play, and destroys in order to play; her dance is one of delight. When we are in delight, free-flowing, following our heart's desires and living them fully in every way, we are in the flow of Shakti. This is your innate, original self, living who you are passionately, and accomplishing your soul's purpose through the flow of Shakti.

The main barriers to Shakti are our culture and upbringing, which include many expectations about how we are to act and behave. The straitjacketing of free expression, the distortion and manipulation around sexuality and love, and the definitions of what is considered acceptable in "polite" society or in politically and spiritually correct circles, is what keeps people's Shakti under wraps.

To express Shakti is to freely be who you are, and all that you can be in your highest potential. The greatest achievements and greatest happiness come to those who are not stopped by what others think about them. Rather, they follow their hearts first and foremost, even if they feel judged for it.

In the past, women abused the power of Shakti, an abuse that lead to the domination, manipulation, and exclusion of men from the realms of power. Our current patriarchal age is a reaction against that separation and domination. Many powerful women from that time are still suffering from this experience, and lie partially disempowered in today's age. Only by men and women coming together can Shakti resurrect in a new way for this age—a way that includes and understands both polarities.

Women are gathering together now to support truth and compassionate means to peace, joy, and equality, not to segregate or judge the masculine, or each other. Such sisterhoods are here to challenge our egos, and to nurture and support our soul's flowering into nonduality, not reinforce the sense of separation from the masculine part of ourselves that we see in reflection in our partners, fathers, and lovers.

Sisterhoods are here to generate Shakti, and in this generation to transmute suffering in both women and men. They can bring forth a new paradigm of giving fully in relationship, of being whole in oneself, of having the soft enduring strength to be patient and deeply compassionate without hunger to get for oneself. Sisterhoods are here to support the flowering of a new consciousness based in equality, a new society based on loving wisdom and harmony between men and women.

This is what true and noble sisterhoods live for, and create. This is what the noblest and most dignified women have created in the past, from the priestesses of Isis to the European Orders of the Black Madonna, to the Tantric priestesses of Asia. This is women's birthright, to reawaken the feminine spirit that is the same in all ages, bringing this spirit into the present and expressing it in joyful and appropriate ways, with power and sanctity.

Shakti is a transformative power that is much needed on the planet at this time, individually, collectively, and by Gaia herself. Shakti harnesses the intelligence and creative power of instinctual sexuality—the flow of vital dynamic life force—with love.

The nature of Shakti cannot be fully defined as it is ever-evolving, ever-expanding, and unique in the way that it flows through each person. This book is merely a guide to Shakti and its flows, and ways to ignite it more fully by actually opening the Shakti Circuit. For each person it will grow, develop, and deepen in unique ways according to your soul's deepest desires. In this ever-expanding universe of our self, change happens all the time.

PART ONE

Pathways to the Womb

The Shakti Circuit

Opening to the Essence of Shakti

THE SHAKTI CIRCUIT HAS BEEN practiced and taught in the Isis Mystery School for thousands of years, and is being revealed now to ignite the renaissance of the Divine Feminine on Earth. As the Shakti Circuit helps to redress the fundamental imbalance between male and female, this renaissance will enable men to step into their Divine Masculine selves even as it enables women to reclaim the loving power of the Divine Feminine.

THE EIGHTEEN PATHWAYS

The eighteen pathways of the Shakti Circuit are pathways of love, power, and wisdom flowing through the body, connecting each human being in the physical world through many dimensions of consciousness to the Galactic Womb, or Galactic Center. The eighteen pathways are how Shakti flows through us. Each woman's womb, and each man's hara, is a gateway to the Galactic Womb. Each of us holds this gateway within us.

Each of the eighteen pathways is a physical point in the body that acts as a bridge, a connector, between your soul, your bodymind, and your emotions. When all eighteen pathways are cleared and merged together in one flow, you experience the essence of deep, feminine meditation in your body. The full expression of loving life force is allowed, as we fully utilize the body to go into the formless, rather than trying to escape the body.

These pathways are how we can transform energy. Each individual pathway leads to certain states of consciousness that you can directly experience for yourself. Each pathway has to be met and mastered; then you surrender, and allow it to master you. In the process of encountering, mastering, and being mastered by all eighteen pathways, Shakti will be fully embodied within you, and the pathways will merge to activate the womb of the Galactic Center, transforming you forever.

Any potential for transformation occurs through awareness, through being aware that there is duality present in the moment. This can lead to a choice to dissolve that duality through a remembrance and expression of unity, by using any of the eighteen pathways. You have the power, in the moment, to do this *at any time*.

Duality is an artful reminder of how we can be whole. When we are reminded of duality in our own life, thoughts, actions, and relationships, we are reminded also of our own innate nature of unity. Duality becomes our greatest ally, our greatest friend, in serving to show us the moments when we are not aligned to love. We then have the wonderful opportunity to realign ourselves by correcting our mind and our energy flow. Duality becomes the ultimate tool for remembering who we really are, and what we can be, by becoming aware of these moments, these gateways, where any of the eighteen pathways can open the door to love, empowerment, and wisdom.

Each of the eighteen pathways is a guardian that we encounter and master along the Way to fully embodying Shakti. The eighteen pathways lead to this experience: recognizing that the womb of God lies within you. The Grail and all the secrets of creation lie right within your belly. Contemplate this for a moment. Heaven on Earth is a perception, a perception unveiled when we realize what lies right inside of us, not just as a metaphysical platitude, but as an experiential fact we

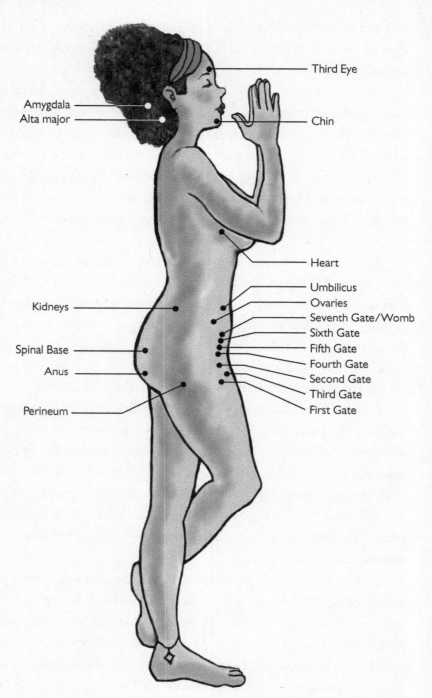

Shakti and its flow—the eighteen pathways

can feel every day. This is an amazing and wondrous reality that we take for granted.

Each time a Circuit completes I stand in awe of the majesty with which God has created us, and marvel at the irony in the simplicity of it all: the cosmic joke in the ways we seek outside of our own temple body to find answers. If we truly knew that the universe lies within us in these eighteen pathways flowing as one, there would be an end to much seeking and striving, and the beginning of an awakened relationship between man and woman.

A woman who knows her power has in her hands the key to her own happiness and success. The source of this power lies within the flowering and ignition of the Shakti Circuit within the body, which is revealed through these eighteen doors, or pathways. These pathways are like a series of portals lying inside you that reveal the universe within.

Close your eyes and imagine this for a moment. Go within the core of your womb/hara, and feel the spaciousness, the vastness there. Now see all the stars, all the planets revolving in this space. Take a moment and feel into your womb: can you visualize this?

Each time you do a Circuit the intensity of the constellations within you increases. You open up to the universe within, and as you do so, the universe outside opens as well. The eighteen pathways reawaken your direct communication and communion with Mother Earth and Galactic Center, something we enjoyed for thousands of years, until this knowledge was lost.

Physically, the eighteen pathways purge, refine, and regenerate you, dissolving old cellular memories and debris, recalibrating your physical body into deeper communion with the other aspects of your being to allow for more thorough embodiment of your soul. Emotionally, the eighteen pathways deepen the excavation and the inquiry, opening the doorways that have been sealed for a long time in the shadows of the dark subconscious to leave no stone unturned.

Mentally, the eighteen pathways bring you into the present moment, deleting old patterns, rewiring the mental body, and relocating your center of gravity away from the mind into its natural place: the womb and heart united, with the mind a servant and ally. The eighteen pathways take the linear mind and shake it up, taking it out of the context of past stories and future hopes or expectations, to dissolve into the present, now, moment. The stories that you hold onto can dissolve, and be recontextualized outside of the pattern of need and mindless chatter. Spiritually, the eighteen pathways are the opening to the map of consciousness, and the container of it.

FEELING SHAKTI

The first movement of creation is Shakti manifesting as pure joy. As you begin to explore the Shakti Circuit by clearing the individual pathways, you will find yourself learning firsthand what Shakti is. This pure flow of Shakti will remind you that your natural state is bliss.

The most powerful creative pulse of the universe is the wave of energy constantly humming behind all life, the throb and tremor that gives rise to all beings. This field of aliveness and transparency is a joy we feel spontaneously undulating throughout all parts of us. It is a bliss that has no reason to be blissful—it just IS.

Shakti has no belief, dogma, or teaching to it, as it is feminine and unique for each person. When we live in the stream of our Shakti, we listen to our body's natural rhythms as they harmonize with the earth, with our loved ones, with the cycles of time and rhythm, and with life itself.

Living in a way that keeps us connected to this core leads to joy. When we allow filters and conditioning to get in the way of this joy bubbling up from deep within us, we lose our creative "spark," and become disconnected from our own vitality, our unique expression of the pulse in all life. Connecting with our bliss is the first step toward living our heart's desires. Feeling the pulse of joy in our own bodies, we align effortlessly with the synchronicity and spontaneity that create nature's processes.

The life spark within all of us becomes conscious when our emotional state is agile and we can easily express our feelings, for emotion = energy in motion. For us to align to this wave requires that we become fluid, and able to experience any feeling whatsoever at any time.

Thus if we can, at will, produce equanimity, delight, love, even anger or tears without charge or attachment to them, then we can be moved from within by the Spirit that is always fluid and open. The less we can summon feelings, the more we are frightened of them, and the more we are at their mercy. Conversely, the more we allow ourselves to experience feelings, the less we can be enslaved by them. If we allow them to pass through us, we become transparent, without charge, not holding on to anything, or anybody.

In this fluid individuality, we learn to move the body, feelings, and mind, so that spirit can move us. We can be any aspect of consciousness at any time, for we are able to feel and express whatever we are needed to be in any given moment, to express all parts of Spirit.

Have you ever had the experience of asking for something and it magically appears within a day or an hour? This is living in the flow of Shakti, for it is already happening; it is manifesting through us.

Shakti is the ultimate transformative force, the movement of the spiral. It flows best with no mind, no hope for the future, no reference to the past. It is the energy of the moment in dynamic, joyful expression. Shakti lives in all eighteen pathways, and when you have connected to each pathway, Shakti wakes up; she ignites. When Shakti flows fully, she dissolves the attachment we have to ideas about who we should be, or who we want to be, or who we might not be, all of which create a constant distraction for the mind. Shakti dissolves these ideas and reveals who we really are.

THE DEEPER MEANINGS OF SHAKTI

Deeper meanings of Shakti are revealed when we break the word into its Sanskrit seed syllables. *Sh, sh,* and *sha* are the seed sounds of the three spirals of creation, known as the three *gunas: sattva, rajas,* and *tamas,* or light, passionate action, and inertia. All three of these sounds are contained in the first syllable of Shakti, so even the word Shakti itself is a Sutra, a code holding within it all that it is. This is why it is important to refer to this power by its proper name, Shakti, rather than saying "life force" or "flow." Power and meaning is held in the utterance of the word itself, especially if you know what it means! This triple spiral is seen in many of the world's sacred traditions, carved on temples generally dedicated to the Goddess. The three spirals symbolize illumination, action, and stability—the action of Shakti as She creates us, the world, and the universe.

The triple spiral

The next seed syllable in the word Shakti is *ka. Ka,* as found in the original Sanskrit primer of The Maheshwara Sutra, means Prakriti, a word that refers to the underlying principle of all motion and creation as being action, desire, the spiraling life force, the innate impulse to grow, birth, and create. Prakriti puts the ideas of the universe into action: it is experience, and the information for experience. Prakriti contains in embryonic form everything that can possibly be experienced, as well as the thing that does the experiencing.

The purpose of Prakriti is to provide you with the enjoyment and lessons of the world, presenting you with experiences that are played over and over, lifetime to lifetime. It is a temporary rather than absolute state, as it arises from nature and is the force of life and death. Once it is played out, it dissolves, and you have an opportunity to use what you learned from it. Prakriti is like a dancer, who, having performed and transformed you through the clarification of your awareness, can leave the stage of this world. When Prakriti is harnessed, made aware of, and mastered, one becomes liberated. She is the both the tool for liberation and bondage to the world at the same time. She leads to being in the world but not of it, enjoying both without attachment, in abundance. Shiva is the master of Prakriti, the Absolute, unmoving, unchanging awareness that sees through her dance.

Prakriti is the substance of the universe, for everything that lives and dies is woven from here. It is the weaving action of life and death, manifesting through the triple spiral. As these three spirals come together they form tetrahedrons (six-pointed stars, as seen in the Sri Yantra*); the network of these tetrahedrons forms the matrix or womb from which creation flows.

Prakriti is the "seed of desire" erupting, bringing all things into fruition, form, action, and dissolution. It is the primordial substance that generates all forms and all experiences through the senses and through the physical form of DNA spirals. In its extremity Prakriti is the chaos that can lead you into the irrational impulse. It is the chaos that divides itself into what has been explored, and what has yet to be explored.

Everything we know has come to us because someone, at some time, explored something unexpected, something unknown, and then

---

*The Sri Yantra embodies in sacred geometry the union of Divine Male and Divine Female energies that harmonize all these spirals into a coherent structure, so there is no longer chaos but order.

The Sri Yantra

shared it with others. This new information comes packaged in risk, fear, excitement at new opportunity, and promise. These emotions can exert an uncanny fascination on your subconscious, bringing to light the depths of your own fears. Within this unknown is the quality that magically transforms one experience into another.

This is when you begin to realize the rules of the game (the Divine Lila), and start to live in it as *I*, the sound vibration and power of Shakti in action.

SHAKTI POWER

As I mentioned earlier, Shakti is a transformative power that we need on the planet at this time because if its ability to harnesses the intelligence and creative power of instinctual sexuality with love. When you bring the instinctual nature of Shakti together with an awareness of the Divine within, the creative potential of God becomes expressed through you, and magnified in your relationships with others. You live it through your sexual attunement to the rhythms and cycles of nature.

Deep within each of us lies this power, an unstoppable primal force. Teeming with life and overflowing passion, this power has its source in the place from which all life pours forth in an inexhaustible torrent. This force can be as scary, as threatening to the control of the mind and small self, as it is loving and nurturing to the soul's freedom. If you have resistance, then chaos and fear is what you will experience. If you have no resistance then you will experience its bliss, which screams "life" to all your senses and soul.

When you encounter such power, you could respond to it in fear, the fear that it will have power and control over you and could destroy you. And it will! It will destroy your resistance to being open, connected, joyful, empowered and free, it will wipe out part of who you think you are, triggering the greatest fear of all: the threat to your very identity. Pure Shakti power cares not for these boundaries, blasting through them. It is freedom, spontaneous and wild, and has no order, structure, or reason to it.

Shakti is the fertile, fecund darkness, the breathing soil of the living earth, the depths of our instinctual nature and intuition. When we allow it to take us, we live in freedom, loving the unpredictability and uncertainty of living in the moment. When we cut ourselves off from this loving expression of power, it consumes us in other ways.

Denying Shakti's flow leads us to overindulge in the external, instead of living according to what lies within us. It leads us to destroy and devour ourselves, creating a desert of consciousness instead of a rich, lush forest of fertile abundance. In reality, we are lusting after something we know we possess, but have forgotten how to tap into. Denying this denies a vital part of our aliveness, our connection to the web of life.

Chaos and powerlessness, disorientation and fatigue, are what the conditioned mind experiences when confronted by the unrestricted energy of Shakti. In the exhaustion that accompanies such a confrontation, the mind can let go of its resistance, relaxing and flowing into the most creative force, releasing into a seething ocean of infinite possibilities, where anything becomes possible.

This is deep, deep nourishment; before words, ideas, even emotions. It shows you how the world is fed. It shows you how, throughout the ages, we have tapped into the power that creates new realities. The unformed, uncontrolled life force lies behind all appearances, all structures, all apparently ordered and reasonable things we do. It is always there as the substratum of life, waiting for us to break the rigidities of what we have created in order to discover what true creation is, moment by naked, vital, pulsing, moment.

Everything is too reasonable! Philosophy, ideas, spiritual systems . . . most of these try to hide away from the force of Shakti, trying to rationalize, spiritualize, and politically correct our most natural of impulses. All of this is done out of fear, and an effort to create an ordered society that denies life, and therefore denies love.

Shakti is love. It leads us to love through its fertile uninhibited force, dissolving all the beliefs that stand in the way of wild joy, the expression of love untrammeled by convention. It says *yes* to love, and connects all life forms, once you have allowed it to flow through you unchecked, and to take you without reservation.

Shakti is a radical force for change, for freedom without boundaries; it is the vital flow of living love itself. Surrendering to this primal love allows you to experience the love that creates all life. And this love is vital for women and men to reclaim. To stand up and have full trust and confidence in who you are, and what you instinctively and passionately feel, means that the whole world can change in a single moment.

Shakti generates energy, power, and strength. Her grit and determination allied with her exuberance, natural intuition, and sovereign authority, enables one to break through any limitations. She is that quality within us that gives us the power to break through old patterns that keep our energy from flowing and manifesting new visions, and following our heart's desires. She is vitality and empowerment. She leads to the breakdown that is the breakthrough.

She can manifest to the mind as dense irrational chaos that is danger, that is radical, that is the essence of risk itself. Without facing this danger, without going to the edge of your experience and beyond, you can never become who you truly are. You have to dive into the deep unknown to know who you are.

The new vision that births through you from this is focused, directed yet expansive. It encompasses and embraces many possibilities, never losing its direction in where it wishes to go. By opening up to all possibilities while remaining grounded, centered, and in your power, you can birth your purpose.

The shadow of Shakti is lust, and addiction to transformation, to seeking, to changing. Passion overflows out of control without the cool detachment of deep contemplation, which yields the immoveable Knowing that absolute truth does not change, and never will. It is important to remember here that Shakti needs Shiva—the Mind of Truth—to guide Her, and to be whole and in Her right place, in harmony. The purpose of transformation is to become and to Be, rather than to eternally process or analyze. Power unleashed generates change, but to integrate this change requires rest. When Shakti is balanced, we can simply rest in being.

THE ESSENCE OF SHAKTI

Shakti flows through both men and women in many ways—in presence, paradox, process, receptivity and resonance, and especially passion.

Presence

Presence is being able to live in the here and now, without judgments about right and wrong or good and bad, and without relying on old concepts about what to do, or not to. Shakti simply responds in the moment and moves to dissolve limitations by using whatever means is appropriate to move the situation or person onward to their next spiral of growth. Sometimes this can be shocking, sometimes loving. It all depends on the unique situation, environment, soul, and relational dynamic you are in. Being present in each of these moments allows more to unfold.

Paradox

Living with paradox involves accepting what appears to be contradictory as two parts of the same whole, dependent on context and the moment of expression. All teachings rooted in truth are unique and individual, responding to the moment. The Buddha would say to one seeker, "There is a God," to another "There is no God." What is good for you in one moment will be bad for you in the next, and the only way to know the difference is to flow in Shakti. This is how spirals of evolution work.

Process

Process and journey can be more valuable than a particular result or destination. In the spiraling journey of life, recognizing the beauty and wonder of each step keeps us flowing, no matter where we are in the process. Staying with each step of our journey, and allowing it to unfold without forcing it, allows us to flow more deeply with Shakti. Awe and wonder keep us open to even larger movements of creation, with laughter providing a direct connection to the beauty of our experiences. We do not necessarily need cathartic or dramatic processing: sometimes healing can be simple and graceful. All that dissolves is resistance, revealing the bliss beyond the pain, and further opening the heart. Being present in each of these moments allows more to unfold.

Receptivity and Resonance

In the flow of Shakti, we feel we are in sync with everything within and around us. The world and our relation to it seem different—our connection to all we perceive is vivid and undeniable. This pulse of perfect rhythm, this synchrony, usually occurs when we are stripped of the boundaries of ego, language, cultural attenuation, and judgment. At this point, it is as if we are involved with the process of creation, instant by instant: we are creating it as it is creating us, for it is always there. We are just too busy in the mind to notice it.

When you are sensitive, you are like a musical instrument, able to resonate with notes coming from within and without, able to surrender to powers greater than yourself. Each person is a symphony of notes playing together in a self-contained harmony. Some people know their tune and resonant frequency, and play it clearly. Such people know themselves well and have had many and varied life experiences; they have many notes to play with, and are able to express freely. They are easy to connect with, and attract others to their music. Other people are more complex and not so easy to understand because they have different chord structures from our own. These are people you might have to spend some time with before you can catch on to their music and "play" with them.

We feel another's music instantly, in our first meeting. We know whether this person resonates with us, whether we are attracted or repelled, whether he or she fits naturally into our own symphony. We can also recognize when someone is being true to his or her own vibration, and is playing it without disguise, pretense, or fakery. To put it simply, your "bullshit" detectors get activated once Shakti flows well through you.

As you are music, you have to work out how to play your tune. What is your keynote on the musical scale? What is the resonant chord that you are most comfortable with? What tempos, what rhythms do you move best to? Maybe some people find it easier to play what other people want to hear from them, as they have not yet discovered the fullness and beauty of their own music.

A large part of your purpose in life is to syncopate, to tune in to these resonant vibrations behind creation. When you get stuck in your life, away from the flow of Shakti, attached or caught in negative patterns, it is because one or more of your sounds is not being heard. When this happens, your music can become frozen, because it is not fully recognized or expressed. To express your music completely—to sound all the notes in your personal symphony—is to free Shakti.

Passion

In the beginning phases of passion, you become easily and enthusiastically inspired to start making bigger changes in your life. Good results start to come from your endeavors, and this fuels you to keep going. Talent, even genius, may be there, but it is only through discipline that you will make anything of it. In this willingness, you say "yes" to life, growth, creativity, and service. You begin to exult in the joy of change, of growth. You follow your heart's desire, a deeper desire than those of the bodymind. You have tasted the divine, and want more. You become a dedicated, passionate human making sure things get done, not just talked about.

Passion is love put into action. It arises when we identify with the spark of life, the will to share in the process of creation. When we experience this passion we seize life; we want to be all of who we are. To become a conscious part of God means you become your unique self, your higher self, for God wants us all to be fully individualized aspects of the One.

This passion is a will to being, a will to share being. It is the love that seeks the well-being of all. It is the action that springs from the deep core of our heart, from where our hidden goodness arises and shows itself in our actions, sharing its joy with others in this dynamic manner. This passion is an urgency to continue evolution, to grow further so we can be more of who we truly are. The universe is expanding as are we, constantly, in every moment. To align to this wave means we continually redefine who we are, in order to embrace and expand to the highest potential available.

Soul passion comes from love. It is passion and love that leads you to enact divine will. Love and passion becomes a force, that when combined with humility and creativity becomes a force for revolution. Evolution becomes the revolution. It is purpose, passion, and love that fuels you, which burns inexhaustibly within you, and pulls you through any, and all, situations. This passion can never be taken away; it is always there. This is the Passion, the conviction that deeply feels for others, and vows to help others, welling up from deep in the core of the heart. This passion for total revolution requires courage, confidence, and honesty.

Passion arises in those who truly love, and will do whatever it takes to live and share more of their love. For when we abandon ourselves to being an evolutionary agent, unlimited energy flows through us. This passion cannot be faked. It is the open willingness to embrace the highest potential in any moment, and to work with others to move that moment forward. It is the catalyst that ignites others marooned in their comfort zones. It is the initiative to dare, to break boundaries, to ignore social mores and etiquette, to break new ground and to break people into this new ground in the most direct way possible. It is the power of clarity that forges open the pathway for evolution to occur.

Deep passion in its evolutionary expression is the urge to bring people together, for the basic pattern of evolution is to unite different elements in order to create something new. Passion for evolution is what brings creative unions together. It is through passion that egos dissolve in creative free flow to form a cohesive unity where souls unite without egoic agendas, beliefs, or feelings of inadequacy. We dissolve boundaries in order to create the next step in evolution, the next big step that we, as humanity, have to take.

When people are masters within themselves, and/or masters of a particular field of expertise, they have inner knowing, and sublime confidence. Then they can delight in meeting with other masters to create something far greater than any of them could possibly achieve alone. The level of light that any single group can bring into the world is limited only by the vision, and thoughts, held in the mind of each of its members.

To do this requires a real thinking-out-of-the-box approach, birthed in the moment, out of Shakti, or "out of the blue." Something simple but radical that has never been done before. Something that links the common threads we all share, regardless of caste, creed, religion, and cultural preferences, and elevates this to a whole new octave. Here we have to experiment with the impossible in order to make it possible, by manifesting it through our own choice, our volunteering to work together as one. This happens through passion, the free flow of Shakti, and our surrender to it.

God makes the world through the processes of evolution, the processes of Shakti, as the impulse, the drive, and the passion to reach and realize God. This evolutionary passion and process of Shakti is reaching to become this image of God that has been planted within all of us. This attraction, this passion, this love, is what makes evolution possible.

ACTIVATING THE PATHWAYS

The full feminine power of Shakti had to be forgotten so it could rise again in a new way for this age, wed with love and the power of the Divine Masculine. Activating the Shakti Circuit can bring many things that block this union to the surface, like dredging up a pot that has not been stirred in a long time. At the bottom of the pot lies all the debris, the half-forgotten shadow remnants and memories of the past that have not yet been digested or assimilated. These memories still have not been brought into the present, their lessons still not learned, the empowerment that arises from them not yet integrated by you.

Activating the Shakti Circuit brings up these memories from earlier in your life and from your past lives: memories of disempowerment, of having shut down your Shakti Circuit in order to survive, even memories of having been persecuted for living with an activated Shakti Circuit. Many of you have these memories, of being persecuted and abused because you had this power of Shakti. In response to the persecution you closed down this feminine power to fit into a mental world, to compete in a mental world, to get by in this world.

Activating the Shakti Circuit allows these memories to emerge, to be seen, embraced, delved into, and particularly to be reclaimed from the darkness. All the times you have denied your power, all the times you have put it to one side to fit in, all the times you have betrayed yourself, all lie in this darkness. This is where you must venture, into the eighteen pathways of the Shakti Circuit within the temple of your body to reclaim this power, and to then express it.

Expressing your power allows more power to arise, more change to occur. This does not mean you should express your power in a dualistic way—as a woman against or in competition with men—but in a powerful and compassionate way.

Negative sisterhoods can keep us stuck in our patterns, for without clarity, compassion, discernment, and the ability to see the whole picture, we become unbalanced, polarized, and judgmental. We ally with the victim consciousness, rather than the liberated, compassionate, and powerful women who see with the eyes of love.

Noble sisterhoods are here to mirror our own needs, to embrace them, and to allow for them without giving in to them. Sisterhoods are here to create a network of women dedicated to truth beyond gender. They have a responsibility to bring themselves and the men in their lives into the womb to heal the pains, the wounds, and the separations we all feel.

This is the power of Shakti, humbly serving others yet still sure, full, and confident in expression, sexuality, and self-contained power. A woman in the flow of Shakti allows herself to be served and taught by men, as men allow themselves to be served and taught by her. Vulnerability is the greatest power, as it leads to love and more Shakti.

We all have our unique purpose in creation. Living that purpose through the action that is Shakti allows us to fulfill ourselves; this, in turn, inspires others to be all that they can be. Raising our standards allows us to change. Action catalyzes, even if it is only a small change every day; it builds on itself.

When reading through each of the eighteen pathways, be honest and open. Which pathways do you still need to encounter and merge with fully? What resistance do you have to embodying each one fully? What do you need to let go of to do this?

Alta Major

The Mouth of the Goddess

I Am the enflamer of truth—the enlivener of the living fire within all things. I Am the never-ending stream of life force, sparking and igniting the spirals within each and every cell of your bodies. I Am the Divine breathing through your body-world. Breathe me in, sound me in, re-member me. Pay heed, with attention and intention, discipline and dedication, to allow my continual pulse and flow to fuel and fire your life, burning away that which no longer serves, creating the fertile ground for birthing the Christ within. (C.O.)

PERHAPS THE MOST IMPORTANT OF the eighteen pathways, along with the womb and heart, is the Alta Major chakra, referred to as the Mouth of the Goddess in the Asian Tantric traditions. Located on the back of the head at the base of the skull, Alta Major is the chakra where Shakti ignites and travels down the spine, sending waves of vibration like a tuning rod throughout your brain, neck, and body. It is the major chakra where the higher aspects of your body of light activate and enter into your physical body.

In ancient Egypt, initiations were given to people through the Alta Major. In many paintings from that culture, the High Priest stands behind the initiate, aiming a copper rod at the Alta Major. This rod transmits sound and also what is known as the "negative green" carrier wave, which sends pulses of pure consciousness into the initiate, turning the whole bodymind into a tuning rod. In these initiations the Alta Major was properly aligned with the rest of the spine, and could therefore conduct vibration easily throughout the whole nervous system and brain in ascending and descending currents of light and Shakti energy. Indeed, the Alta Major was seen as a galactic doorway to these higher forces, a portal to the concentrated, high frequency beams of light that unite the Alta Major and the pineal gland.

Together, the Alta Major and the pineal gland are the seat of your intuition. When you consciously connect into these chakras, you accelerate the embodiment and enlightenment process. The Alta Major is the lunar, feminine entrance to the third eye, as the pineal is the solar, masculine entrance. In most of us, these two entrances to the third eye are disconnected. When both solar and feminine entrances connect via their infinity loops, all the codes that have been waiting in the DNA for thousands of years activate, and express themselves through the throat chakra, literally manifesting our goals, visions, and perceptions.

When the Alta Major is aligned physically and energetically, your physical body and your lightbodies also connect on a deeper level, accelerating the awakening, ignition, and "descent" of your lightbodies into your physical one. The Alta Major, pineal, and the energy flow of the eighteen pathways can now anchor, and flow freely and unimpaired, allowing you to integrate and unite bodymind and spirit here on Earth, and to embody light into matter itself.

> Yet in order to manifest this, the Alta Major dissolves the old, worn-out parts of you, in order to create a new you. As Shakti says, "Wild, sweetly singing, I am joyous in my destruction. I am pure vital life force. I am beyond duality. I will burn through your illusions, burn through your mind. I am your liberation. Feel me now; I do not come softly. My breath is fire. I will melt all resistance in my path." (W.C)

Truth has no convention to it. Sometimes it is not nice, or is politically or spiritually "incorrect." But it is truth nonetheless, and it is this that burns and transforms. It is this that brings us to our self. And it is this enflaming energy that the Mouth of the Goddess ignites.

I am the threshold, the doorway for the return of the Divine Feminine. Knowledge of my import and presence had been hidden away until such time when all was in alignment for the re-membering and re-awakening of the pathways of Isis. I am the focal point, the Alpha and Omega for these pathways. I am your connection to the vaster cosmos. Clear out the clutter of held patterns, thought-forms, and imbalances and I will open you to the higher realms of knowing. There is great power held here.

I am the portal through which Shakti courses, and when clear I hold the power to transmute the finer vibrations of the higher realms into manifestation and action. Open yourself past the mind to the unfathomable, past your own knowing and I will flourish. This deep pulsing energy of the wild mother is my life-blood.

Your first breath of life coming through me can be uncomfortable to get used to when for so many years you have breathed and found your center in a different way. When you learn to breathe through me and center yourself in your Circuit, this will change everything and bring you "off-balance," which is actually putting you into true balance.

I want your focus to always start with me. I am the beginning and the end of the Circuit. I hold connection points, trigger points for all aspects of the Shakti Circuit—like the feet of the human body mirrors all of its organs and meridians. You will find as you work more and more with me, and open up the pathways to a greater degree, that even one focused breath into me will ignite the full Circuit. (T.A.)

The Alta Major holds the seed of manifestation. Manifestation is the ability to transmit the spark of love, wisdom, or power through your thought or Presence. Manifestation is not just about manifesting things outside of yourself: it is about manifesting the Divine within.

This inner, deeper manifestation will not wilt with time or age; it will always be with you, as you will be living it through your thoughts, feelings, and actions. You will become the Divine in every moment, and through your presence will transmit it wherever you go.

In order for us to manifest the Divine, we have to stand in perfect harmony with the life frequency. This means that any negative, depressed thought, any doubt, any fear, will negate the power to give life. Thus, the promise of being able to manifest with our thoughts cannot happen until the Alta Major is healed. Manifestation is power, and power will only come if there is balance to create harmony, so that what is created is for the greatest good.

The potential to be all you can be is the promise of the Alta Major, the Mouth of the Goddess. There is nothing outside of yourself; all aspects are within you. The more you are connected and aligned, the more of yourself can come into your present experience of life. It is through Presence, not through objects, that we experience the Divine. This is manifestation. To reflect the Divine, we have to become aware of, embrace, and include the animal aspect of ourselves. Successfully cultivating the Witness Consciousness allows the full power of manifestation to bloom when aligned with the rest of the Shakti Circuit.

Light and sound adjustments to the brain and the Shakti Circuit can help you rapidly open the Alta Major. However, this can be traumatic, as it can propel you into the universal subconscious mind at a rapid rate. This is not recommended unless you have ongoing support with an experienced guide of these realms. If this guidance is available, then rapid evolutionary steps can lead you to galactic consciousness. This involves a direct recognition that we are the galaxy. We take this on through our own beings; we become a conscious part of our galaxy.

The temptation of the Alta Major is to get lost in the galactic unconscious; this can manifest in sometimes quite bizarre encounters, dreams, unusual coincidences, as well as strange lethargies, weight gains to protect yourself and your womb, and a general lack of energy, because it is draining from you.

The Alta Major, the Mouth of the Goddess, has been a very secret chakra, as it holds for us the power to co-create as divinely conscious beings. This requires great courage, and the willingness to take the greatest risks, to go beyond the norm and into the deepest unknown. It also means we have to die to what we have known in many ways.

LIFE AND DEATH

Shakti reveals death as part of life, intimately interconnected. A simple law of nature is that for something new to be born—be it a new you, a new way of being, a new way of relating, and/or a new society, culture, or government—something has to die. Something has to die in you for you to truly grow. Something has to be destroyed on this planet for a new culture, and new planet, to arise. When humanity learns this lesson, then new forms of creating can arise that are in a natural grace with the cyclic flows of the feminine, and deaths of old forms can happen in less traumatic and dramatic ways.

This power, which can be seen as magical, is what many fear, and are also attracted to simultaneously. Shakti brings forth the deepest polarities, the wildest extremities, in order to harmonize them into flow. The path of eternal life is very much one of death, indeed of progressive and successive deaths, which become subtler and subtler, more and more graceful, as one progresses. Shakti leads you to a good death, reminding you that you are mortal, reminding you to get up and experience life now, as it is. With death on your shoulder, you cannot ignore life or what it presents you with any longer. Absence reminds you of the amazing potential for total presence; and this is what the best spiritual teachers do, reveal their absence to facilitate you into Presence, or bewilderment as the case may be!

Shakti holds life and death in each hand, as personified by the Hindu goddess Kali. She holds a space for life to reveal, create, and generate itself, and she holds a space for death to conceal, dismantle, and dissolve forms and ideas. You can experience this spaciousness by holding your breath between your inhalation and exhalation for certain periods of time. When you do this for long enough, you experience this point between life and death, and the fear that lies there also. The inherent threat and thrill of the point where life meets death is dangerous, radical, scary, holy, and sacred; here Shakti acts as the bridge to full empowerment. Those who dare to bridge life and death are the most radical of all, and it is these people who act as way showers, as guides, for birthing into eternal life.

SHAKTI AS DESTROYER

Shakti provokes and is provocative. She teases, tempts, triggers, and catalyzes in order to bring more true, grounded love into your human life, here on Earth now; not in the future, not in the past, but in the naked, searing intensity of the present moment where we are continually being born in every nanosecond. Being born in every moment can take us to the brink, the edges of light and dark, and ultimately into love. Here there is no mind, and the reasons for our service to others become exposed—whether we operate out of guilt, shame, and fear, or the need to feel good or loved to fill up a hole within ourselves, or something else. Shakti brings us to clarity amid the chaos, by taking us deep into the chaos where clarity hides.

> *I Am the volcano waiting to burst, to burn, disintegrate, dissolve that which stands between humanity and god. I Am ultimate compassion that knows that in order for the Divine to truly arrive on this planet destruction has to happen . . . the phoenix cannot be born until he burns to ashes. My service is not always easy, nice, or soft, but always giving, giving of truth. (T.A.)*

Pure Shakti was demonized by patriarchal orders out of fear that this power could not be controlled, and therefore it became synonymous with demons and the dark. Shakti is a source of fear for many men, as it leads them out of the transcendent state and back into normal human life with its cares and concerns, back into matter, into form.

When you can rest in the full flow of your Shakti you are in true Presence. True Presence has no mind: it is without barriers, preference, fear, or belief of any kind.

Unencumbered by the weight of light and dark, right or wrong, my vision is clear. I aim to destroy your smallness. The full power of my Shakti blasts through any resistance to being in the unlimited, unfathomable power of now. This can be dark. This can be hell. It is only your idea of hell. It is only your fear. Your aversion to power, to death. Your attachment to your ideas keeps you bound. RESISTANCE is your death. I've come to liberate. Be forewarned: your death will be your life; your darkness, your deepest joy. Surrender to me. Surrender—and find your bliss. (W.C.)

AGNI SHAKTI: THE FIRST FLAME OF CREATION

The spark of all life begins in the primordial waters, the oceans of light and sound that comprise our universe. This spark, found in the core of all life forms, is the first light of consciousness, the first flame of Shakti. In India this is called Agni Shakti.

Agni is found in these primordial waters and was seen and heard by the Vedic Seers, who described it as being accompanied by the sound of bellowing cows. This sound was not literally cows, but was described as such by the mountain-dwelling Seers as they had no context for what the sound actually was—the sound of whale song. The Vedic Seers understood that these cows or whales hold the codes of creation; they heard the sounds as they "saw" in their minds the processes of life being born, just as they saw the syllables of the Sanskrit alphabet glistening and forming the tree of life.

The Seers also saw that all sound is spherical in nature, and that Agni dwells in the heart of the sphere of sound, the sphere of life. The deepest forms of Agni lie in the soul, the flame hidden within our hearts, which is also a power that pervades all of nature, and the first spark of creation arising from Galactic Center. There is an Agni in the rocks, an Agni in the plants (the power of photosynthesis), and an Agni in animals (their digestive fire)*.

We are all forms of Agni. We are living flame walking around within form.

As human beings, we are the intelligence of fire and light, and Agni is this spark of fire and light within each of us. Agni Shakti is the power of the phoenix, the sacred fire of pure and perpetual creativity that dissolves and creates. This power enters us through the Alta Major chakra, then circulates throughout the whole Shakti Circuit. Spiritual practice can develop Agni on all levels of consciousness, opening up the eighteen pathways to allow the sacred fire to flow unimpeded throughout all parts of you and into the heart fire, the sacred fire of your soul.

These spiritual practices include physical yoga and dietary practices to purify and balance the digestive fire (Jatharagni), *pranayama* or breathing practices to purify, refine, and energize the breath fire (Pranagni), *dharana* or concentration to focus the fire of the mind (Manasa-agni), and *dhyana* or meditation to increase the fire of penetrating insight and wisdom (Buddhi-agni).

In addition, Samadhi describes the practice of one-pointed focus on the central point within the brain, until it merges into divine fire to effect transformation on a soul level (Jiva-agni). Jnana Yoga, the yoga of insight and knowledge, illuminates ignorance through the light of wisdom (Jnana-agni). Bhakti Yoga, the yoga of loving devotion, transmutes lust into the fire of Love (Prema-agni). Karma Yoga dissolves self-centeredness in the passion of selfless service (Seva-agni). Raja Yoga, the integral yoga of meditation, burns conditioned habits and the supremacy of ego in the fire of Samadhi.

---

*From a passage by David Frawley on Agni Ayurveda in *Yoga and the Sacred Fire: Self-Realization and Planetary Transformation* (Twin Lakes, Wis.: Lotus Press, 2004).

A powerful form of fire alchemy is the sounding of the 1008 mantras of Agni, the sound and light of Shakti. She moves in the moment, and creates more radical beauty by clearing away the dead wood of the old. She is perpetually moving and continually birthing in each and every moment, allowing us to continually recreate ourselves, and to birth anew.

THE ATLAS: THE PHYSICAL ASPECT OF THE ALTA MAJOR

The atlas is the first vertebra of the spine, the connection between the spinal cord and the brain. In Greek mythology, Atlas is a Titan and demigod condemned to forever carry the world upon his shoulders (as a punishment from Zeus for daring to challenge him). His back and neck are compressed by the weight as he stoops over, crushed by his heavy burden. Atlas means "he who suffers," "the bearer," or "endurer." Ninety-nine percent of us are born with this skeletal atlas defect that keeps us trapped in the bodymind, and in stress patterns that prevent more energy from traveling down from the Alta Major to the rest of our central nervous system and bodymind.

To open up the Alta Major Chakra and allow Shakti to circulate and flow freely throughout the eighteen pathways, a physical adjustment to the atlas is usually necessary.* The atlas alignment was discovered in 1993 by disabled Swiss doctor René-Claudius Schuemperli. In his research, Schuemperli found that several advanced cultures of antiquity, particularly the Mayan and Egyptian cultures, regularly practiced manual repositioning techniques of the atlas. He further discovered that the atlas is probably dislocated within almost all humans from birth, which can entail a chain reaction of symptomatic complaints, such as back problems, migraines, psychological complaints, complaints of the neck, spinal column, knee, and hip joints.

---

*Please see the resources section on page 229 to access more information on the atlas and to see where you can receive an atlas adjustment.

This has a direct effect on the psyche and organs, since this disconnection disturbs internal body communication, and disrupts the whole nervous system, which becomes unable to send out its signals to the bodymind at optimum value. This disconnection prevents the descent of light down the spine, and the ascending current of kundalini energy up the spine.

Our bodies compensate and adjust to the incorrect position of the atlas from birth, creating a false body attitude. This incorrect positioning causes a disturbance of the sensitive, static equilibrium of the spinal column. By the correction of the dislocated atlas, this chronic and long-disturbed internal communication can return to perfect function in the nerve channels on all levels. As the atlas is fixed to the suspension of the spinal column, the body's own healing forces activate to decrease stress responses and increase centering.

This makes the bodymind freer, lighter, and more fluid. Organs and skeleton realign, old tension patterns dissolve, posture changes, and more energy is available to all parts of you. This is because the central nervous system is now able to transmit and receive energy at 100 percent efficiency throughout the whole body, mind, and soul.

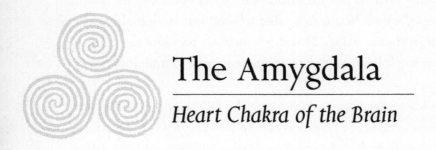

The Amygdala

Heart Chakra of the Brain

WHILE THE EIGHTEEN PATHWAYS CAN be accessed in any order, the most powerful ways to access them arise from the womb and its gates, the Alta Major, and the heart. This book presents them in a circuit that begins with Shakti flowing through the Alta Major at the back of the head, to then run down the spine, around to the yoni and womb, then up the front of the body. Each one is a doorway to specific states of consciousness, and each one invites to you to explore the feelings, power, love, and wisdom that are stored within.

Deep in the base of the oldest, reptilian part of the brain, lies nestled the amygdala. This almond-shaped organ is the feeling, emotional heart of the brain, and is one of the eighteen pathways of the Shakti Circuit. It is the same shape as the middle section of the *vesica piscis,* the shape that depicts the first movement of creation, the first movement of Shakti.

The amygdala detects danger or emotion associated with past experiences from childhood and/or past lives that were stamped within the brain as being dangerous, or emotionally significant. If the amygdala detects incoming stimuli that match these stamps, then it alerts us to potential dangers by pumping increased levels of stress hormones and neurotransmitters throughout the body and brain. Almost anything connected with the original event (an accent, a sound, a picture, a per-

34

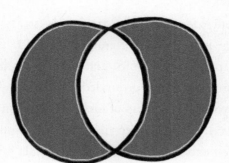

Vesica piscis

son, a dream, a conversation, a relationship dynamic) can trigger a flash-back of the experience.

Past traumas, emotional memories, and barriers to our deepest fulfillment are stored in the amygdala and can be perpetually retrig-gered, keeping us in vicious cycles of reaction. Amygdala dysfunction affects our ability to open fully to joy and happiness. One of its main symptoms is an avoidance of darkness. Indeed, being overly attracted by "the light," or becoming light polarized and fearing darkness is a sure sign the amygdala needs healing! Much New Age culture is predicated on this. Other signs of an out-of-balance amygdala include fear, panic attacks; our mouths and yonis may go dry; we need prescription drugs to be calm; we have an inability to experience and fear of orgasm; lack of joy; fear of death, fear of life; feelings of depression, helplessness, and disempowerment.

When the amygdala is not working at its optimum, there is a gap between who we feel ourselves to be, and who we think ourselves to be. In this gap lies the inability to articulate what we are thinking and feel-ing on deeper levels. It is in this gap where much disempowerment and frustration can occur, for when you connect what you are deeply feeling to your expression of it, your sense of identification can also shift.

The amygdala creates a sense of emotional identification that keeps you emotionally grounded, and emotionally secure. This security can be a double-edged sword, however; we may be safe but imprisoned within our conditioned environment and responses. It is easy to become comfortable with what has served you emotionally thus far; it is more of a challenge to go beyond this point and strive for a higher emotional resonance, an expression that is grounded in the soul and spirit.

In moving beyond these layers of identification, one's sense of emotional well-being shifts to a higher vibration that embraces more love, and deeper heartfelt expression. When the amygdala is healed, we think with our hearts, and feel with our minds.

The amygdala, which works in conjunction with the hypothalamus, is a major pleasure center, containing both opiate-producing neurons and opiate-receptive neurons, which together generate feelings of numbness and a narcotic high. They also help to generate more serotonin production, serotonin being the hormone of ecstasy. Together, these two organs contribute to the production of sexual feelings, as well as unusual and fearful phenomena including out-of-body, hallucinogenic, and dream-like states that involve sex, religion, and the experience of God. It is the amygdala that enables us to experience emotions such as love and religious rapture, as well as the ecstasy associated with orgasm, and the dread and terror of the dark unknown.

"Fear the Lord your God."—Deuteronomy 10:12

Many who encounter "God" or "angels" also commonly experience fear. We are repeatedly told in the Bible that to know fear is to know God, with a combination of both fear and exaltation usually being termed religious awe. The amygdala makes it possible to experience all of these things at the same time, not just spiritual and religious awe, but all the terror and dread of the unknown. And yet, it is also the amygdala that is responsible for the capacity to transcend the known by the union and harmonious dance of polarities—the extremes of light and dark, angelic and demonic, sexual and spiritual all combining in one flow.

The amygdala, when healed, is the uniter of the primal polarities and extremes—the breaker of taboos and judgments about the sexual force, and the nature of love. The fear, anxiety, panic, excitement, visions of demons, fear of going into the unknown, all contrast with their opposites in the amygdala: ecstasy, peace, transcendence, fulfillment, deep healing, affection, love, visions of angels and God. All of this is held within the amygdala and its connection to the womb and yoni and all these polarities have to be felt, experienced, and unified in order to open up fully to the Divine in all its aspects. Strangely enough, the amygdala is similarly named to Mary of Magdala (Magdalene)—the feminine, heart-centered aspect of Shakti, the sexual partner of the Divine Masculine.

The Gnostic poem "Thunder Perfect Mind" illustrates these polarities perfectly, as do many Tantric paths.

> For I am the first and the last.
> I am the honored one and the scorned one.
> I am the whore and the holy one.
> I am the wife and the virgin.*

The experiencing of the extremes of darkness and light in order to reach enlightenment is something we all have to do in order to reach the "middle way." If you have not already experienced such extremes, you will; if not in this lifetime, then in others.

Stress on the amygdala affects the feminine part of you that holds memories of having separated from the masculine qualities of strength, courage, power, and will. It affects the masculine part of you that holds memories of having separated from the feminine qualities of nurturing, empathy, tenderness, and kindness. The amygdala is the center that controls emotions in the duality of love or fear, reaction or peace.

Healing this center in your body is vital to expanding your level of consciousness. Activation of the amygdala increases your levels of emotional openness and love, and is vital to your well-being, for the amygdala is the heart chakra of the brain. When it opens, light and love

---

*From the Nag Hammadi Library, Dead Sea Scrolls.

radiate to the other brain centers, and the whole brain starts to heal.

The amygdala governs heart-wisdom and emotional intelligence. It is connected to our ability to respond rather than react in the present moment to precisely what is occurring. When the amygdala is healed and opened, we are free from the fight-or-flight reaction. The heart opens more, permeating our bodies with feelings of warmth and love. Making love with an open amygdala is an experience that takes love-making to a whole new octave.

To open the amygdala to its full potential requires that we travel into our greatest dualities, judgments, and taboos—the secrets we hide deep within the subconscious, released by the anus and the kidneys. Many of these hidden judgments involve sexuality and ecstasy, and/or their polar opposites of fear of the dark, repression, and denial. We have to willingly explore these deepest anxieties about ourselves, and bring them into recognition, acceptance, and resolution. Opportunities for healing the amygdala can be found on www.christblueprint.com, the website listed in the resource section at the end of this book.

Transforming Anger into Bliss

The Clarity of the Kidneys

WHEN WE BRING OUR INNER polarities into harmony, the anger and suffering we feel within (as well as what is directed at us from others) can transform into bliss. This transformation is very much a function of Shakti, for wherever she goes and whatever she does, she has joy etched into her features. This may seem strange, transforming anger and rage into bliss and laughter, yet this is the dance of polarities in action, and was a hallmark of both Magdalene and Christ.

Anger is energy, Shakti in a different form, waiting to be known for its true nature. Learning to honor anger is a key here. Once we honor and listen to our anger, it may still arise, but will be felt in a different way. As this happens a switch can ignite in your energy system, and the anger becomes joyful, even funny in its expression. This is a natural expression and flow of Shakti that anyone can experience, as anger is Shakti, just in a raw form.

In this feeling, you become able to transform and transmute whatever is thrown at you. Instead of becoming defensive and springing to a retort based on fear or anger, you may feel a burst of joyous compassion arising to meet the anger, and in so doing will short-circuit and dissolve it. And this can be fear's greatest healing sometimes: to provoke a response so alien to what we are programmed to receive, that it generates a completely new outlook. In this process, you may also start to become a magnet for catalyzing others and bringing out their shadow sides, which crave being seen, and reclaimed.

Try this one day the next time a friend or a partner gets mad at you: compassionately, from your heart, laugh. Share joy loudly. Make sure you do not laugh *at* the person; do not mock them, but express joy so they are reminded of what lies underneath the anger. What happens?

To be able to use the polarities of anger and joy without judgment allows us to assume many forms in order to dissolve fear and anger by encountering them directly. The energy behind anger can manifest as irritation, deep hurt, guilt, shame, resentment, fear, and/or impatience. This anger can be put into focused action through physical exercise. It can also be fully experienced through conscious relationship and lovemaking, which transmutes emotions and pushes you through many barriers.

When channeled, anger becomes fuel for willpower. It can help you stretch beyond the limits of your body, mind, and emotions. Bringing emotions into physical exercise deepens the process and makes it an alchemy of grounding. It can strengthen positive emotions and can take you deeper on a journey into negative ones and help you come to terms with them, and work with them directly as pure life force.

Bringing emotions into exercise spiritualizes the body. It opens the channels for your emotions, body, and lightbodies to connect here on Earth, in pulsing vitality and calm, centered presence. Exercise helps you to embody by bringing Heaven to Earth in your physical being. This can mean going to the gym, lifting weights, running—anything that pushes your physical body.

The willingness to feel all the emotions is the key: the irritation, deep hurts, guilt, shame, resentment, fear, and impatience. Then they can be worked with physically, as they are lodged within the body. Merging blocked emotions or sources of irritation or anger with the physical in a dynamic way can open you to embrace these parts of yourself.

Similarly, when making love, these powerful energies can be put into practice for healing. Simply, but sacredly, prepare your bed and your intent for this healing. One of you should generate your deepest anger, and make love in this way. This can be angry love, or just the person feeling it within but making love lovingly. When you swap, those who have the greatest fear can then allow themselves to be penetrated, and surrender into feeling their deepest fear while being penetrated. If the partner who feels the most fear is the man, he can allow the woman to ride and energetically penetrate him, surrendering to her power.

This is a simple practice, but very effective. When you are naked, there is nowhere to hide, no intellect to rationalize. You are in the moment, intimate, and already vulnerable. First you generate an emotion, then you move it with your lovemaking into expression and manifestation, and finally, transmutation. In this process, you discover deeper levels of the emotion, and may also experience incredible lovemaking accompanied by passion, compassion, and love. This practice heightens intimacy in a relationship, and brings each partner to a deeper understanding of the other in a visceral way.

When you are fluid and open, ready to allow Shakti to flow through you and ready to transform whatever emotions arise, you move directly into all the things you do not wish to face, and then on into awakened blissful states. To be both fierce and gentle, compassionate and wrathful, kind and powerful is the ultimate paradox. Being able to experience all faces of light and dark equally, and able to recognize the gifts that light and dark hold, is what Shakti brings to us. And this is a boon for a suffering planet.

THE KIDNEYS

The kidneys represent feminine clarity and flow, as they are the *chi* circulators of the body. Working with our kidney energy helps us to transform fear and anger into bliss, embracing our feminine energy. If we are nervy, stressed, overreactive, or scattered, it may very well be the kidneys that need cleansing, balancing, and restoring.

The kidneys hold much of the fear stored in our bodies, for the kidneys run on the water element. Their color is sky-blue, like the sky on a perfect cloudless day. They recycle energy, filtering and recirculating it in processes of restoration and revitalization.

The kidneys also generate much of the chi in our bodies, and have a role in distributing it appropriately. For instance, the kidneys help to pull excess masculine or mental energy from the head back down to the belly and womb, our natural center of gravity. They redistribute feminine energy to wherever it needs to be, to places that have been stuck or stagnant. The energy that has been previously rooted in the masculine mind, caught up in confusion, projection, and stress, can now become clear and relaxed.

The kidneys speak: We serve as the storehouse and filtering station for all that flows through your body. We are connected to all that is feminine. Relax the mind, breathe into me, and practice trust. We filter the energies coming in and moderate them to the different parts of the Shakti Circuit and body. So, we are like a transfer station. Some parts of your body are ready to hold higher frequencies than other parts of your body. Until they all come into alignment, we can step these energies down, and slowly build up those parts little by little, allowing the higher frequencies to come through as they can handle them. We are master coordinators of the entire body system.

It is important to keep us clear, and breathe directly into us through the Kidney Breath so that we can operate at our highest capacity for you. We work especially hard when you are transmuting in healing work. At these times, we need even more cleansing breath. Breathe in to us daily. We have been held in fear for so long. And yet we have such nourishment to bring you. (T.A.)

⚘ Kidney Breathing

Stand outside in nature. This exercise will be particularly powerful if you are under a cloudless blue sky and by a water source, such as a pool or the ocean.

1. Place your feet parallel to each other, as in a Tai chi stance. Bend your knees and keep your spine straight.
2. Formulate an intention, for instance, "Clear the fear from my kidneys, and make me aware of what that fear is." Speak your intention out loud three times.
3. Relax your perineum and bottom.
4. Place your hands behind you, over your kidneys, which are situated either side of your lower back, with palms facing upward. The sides of your index fingers should be against your back.
5. Breathe deeply, yet gently, into the kidneys for 10 minutes. Imagine blue energy flowing into the kidneys through your palms, energizing and revitalizing them.

You may feel heat, tingling, sweating, and shaking as the energy starts to flow through you. Listening to soothing water-based music will also help during the practice.

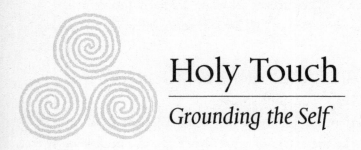

Holy Touch

Grounding the Self

ONE OF THE FIRST THINGS we experience in life is the sense of touch. Touch is what connects us to each other, and to the felt experience of love. A hug is worth a thousand words.

Touch is common to almost all we do, including physical handling, emotional and mental grasping, as well as touching ideas and concepts. Touch links awareness and sensitivity; without it, the senses cannot communicate or interrelate. When we are "in touch" with our feelings, and when we are "touched" by an experience, we are moved and inspired to go beyond our limits. We can have a "light touch" or a "heavy hand," for touch is how we reach out to people, how we are recognized in life, and how we recognize others. When we just want to feel another's presence, we say we are "touching in" or "touching base."

Touch is what creates and sustains relationships in the web of life. When we reach out and touch another, we are reaching for information, experience, connection, and feeling. Without touch we would be sterile and unemotional beings, for touch links and connects you to me, and our bodies to each other. Touch connects one thought to the next, one emotion I am feeling to the one you are feeling, one part of my world to another. We understand one another by touching the same link in each other, by striking the same key in each other. Touch is how we connect, give, and receive. In this connection we can feel life itself.

Touch is what opens the heart. When we touch our feelings deeply, our pains and sadness can arise through this vulnerability. Touch brings more intimacy to our lives, more real sharing. When we are truly touched, and touch another, walls of belief and pain can dissolve, and love arise. If we miss touch, then we feel as though we are missing a part of ourselves.

Touch heals. Touching another with sacred intent can provide healing, blessing, and comfort; it is a way to share more love. The intimacy and affection this brings can break down barriers as we realize that we are loved and loving beings. This ability of touch to heal has been the foundation of many healing practices and religious rites, including those at Delphi and in ancient Egypt.

Another aspect of holy touch is a simple transmission of the Divine Mother's grace from one womb to another through belly-to-belly touch. The woman who is the vessel for this transmission should be clear, with all her *nadis* and meridians active. In this sacred exercise, the forgotten or neglected womb feels the direct presence of love again in her power center; her source of creativity reawakens to heal ancient wounds and memories.

This is a simple direct transmission through touch that opens up gateways to deeper healing. In this grace you receive exactly what you need, whatever serves your highest potential and the flowering of your womb. With one simple touch Shakti appears, sharing her Presence with you. Ammachi spreads this grace with hugs, while other spiritual healers lay hands on the head or the womb, or gaze into another's eyes.

In the past, the Priestesses of Pythia at the Oracle at Delphi used to heal through touch and being touched, as did the Priestesses of Isis. At Delphi, they used to draw the vapors emanating from the earth into their yonis and then up into their wombs. As they did this the gases, combined with the unique geomagnetic properties of the earth at Delphi, stimulated their wombs and opened their seven gates so that the voice of prophecy could be heard—the voice of the womb. The power of the womb was applied in healing touch as well.

THE BASE OF THE SPINE

Touch connects us to the base of the spine, which is our physical foundation, our place of stability and grounding. It is our strength and our source of security and support in the world. The base of the spine centers and anchors our physical structure, and is the root of our selves. It is literally and figuratively where we sit. Without it we are rootless, and cannot ground higher energies.

When you are disconnected from the base of your spine, many fears arise. You feel that you must get what you need from others because you are unable to feel secure within yourself. Abundance issues center around the spinal base, as well as fears of abandonment and of being alone. In a recent UK survey, over 60 percent of women in married couples said they would leave their marriage today if they had their own money.* These women are not in the marriage for love; they are in it for the spinal base—the security and comfort not found in themselves that they therefore seek in others.

Conversely, when the spinal base is clear and connected, we feel sturdy, grounded, and able to act in the world. We feel calm, secure, and connected to our own abilities, so we move forward without fear, knowing we are supported. In this state of rootedness, we are able to safely ascend into our higher chakras. In fact the more we are grounded, the further we can reach into the realms of light. We are like a tree: the more rooted we are in the spinal base, the more our branches can stretch up and connect to the sky.

The spinal base is one of the five centers of the root chakra, connected to the seat of kundalini, or Shakti energy, that lies coiled there. The other four are the anus, the perineum, the yoni/lingam, and the clitoris/tips of the lingam. When the spinal base is clear and active, it allows the ascent of kundalini up the spine. If this channel is not clear, or is unstable, the ascent of kundalini will burn and traumatize different parts of your emotional, physical, and spiritual bodies.

The Times of London, January 2008.

♣ A Five-Minute Meditation for Grounding

There are many practices for opening, grounding, and connecting to the spinal base. The following is one that you can do easily:

1. Sit on the ground and rock on your spinal base. Feel it. Focus on it, and breathe deeply into it for 8 long breaths.
2. Place a tennis ball under the base of your spine and breathe into it.
3. Move the ball gently around the base of the spine.

What happens and what do you feel? Breathe into, and release, any tension.

THE BIG RELEASE

The anus is another center of the root chakra, and perhaps the most taboo part of our bodies. It is perceived as a dirty place we hide, an unnameable thing not to be mentioned. The anus is the carpet under which we sweep our shame, shadow, and fear so they do not see the light of day. For here is literally where our shit is; what we do not wish to see, what we do not want to know, or admit, about ourselves. In Indian medicine the anus and its flow of energy is known as *apana,* the downward pulling stream of energy in opposition to the pure life force of *prana,* or chi. Apana rules all excretory or release functions, and has an outward movement, acting like a release valve through which our emotional, physical, and mental waste can flow out. In this release of negativity, we "let go" of toxic emotions, unneeded foodstuffs, mental habits, and relationship debris that is no longer required for our evolution.

Apana's importance to our well-being is significant, as without releasing the old we cannot move ahead with the new; we cannot evolve or live fully to our highest potential. Apana is seen as master of the body, without which we would die; for if we cannot release the old toxins, beliefs, and wounds that block us, then we literally suffocate.

Because the anus is one of the five points that make up our root chakra, its openness is fundamental to the free flow of Shakti. Without the release and letting go that the anus allows us, we can never fully connect to Shakti.

It is also vital to clear, heal, and open the anus in order to open the womb, as they are interconnected. The more open the anus, the more we are able to surrender to the pathway between the yoni and the womb, and the more we are able to receive and create. With an open anus we are able to feel and express more clearly; we deeply experience our own judgment and aversion to things within us, which might then get reflected to the outside.

People with tight anuses are controlling, fearful, and judgmental in their attitude and approach to life, and to other people. Notions of political and spiritual "correctness" arise from this area being closed. In many ancient societies including the Essene cultures and Tantric societies worldwide, the cleansing of the anus was of paramount importance, and led to the development of enemas, colonics, and specific exercises.

The first aspect of the healing of the anus is all about exposing your fears, shames, and judgments, and then letting go of them. To stop being "anally retentive," to let go of contracted and closed-minded attitudes, is one of the hardest things to do, whether you need to let go of habits, fears, or shame or let go of fixed ideas, people, and beliefs that have served you until this point, but can no longer take you where you need to go in order to become all that you can be. Excretion, or letting go, is an archetypal quality that we all share. It is part of the element of water, the governor of the anus, which lets go of stagnant material—whatever is no longer useful—to merge into a more fluid form.

Truly, I'm furious. Lifetimes I've given away my power and my bliss. Lifetimes I've abandoned myself. I feel the anger; the rage and resentment. And at the same time, the fear of force and the brutality of other's untamed power. Of my own. Out of this comes the contraction. Visceral. A tight clenching in the body of my anus held like a turning away from life. And

so it is: the need to control and protect myself from the pain of this hurt;
or its memory. Beyond these things lurks the basic fear. Slippery, skulking,
cowardly. So simple really. So inanely obvious.

At the root of all contraction and all resistance to flow, mine is a deep
lack of trust of what may come with surrender. And within this I feel the
need born from the fear. Through the continuation of breath, slowly, there
comes a feeling of peace, of allowing life—for a moment—to flow fully
through me. And with the last exhale, I feel myself falling into a stillness
of being. And also, uncovering a sadness in my heart. Grief. My mom. My
mother. Physically and metaphorically my connection to the feminine. It
feels like a place of coming home to the trust, love, and surrender—into
the source of my creation and sustenance. (A.T.)

Letting go, like water, implies transparency. Everything flows through you, and you hold onto nothing. There is no reaction, no past to irritate or stimulate you into action or reaction. Indeed, all reaction comes from the past, whether it's a past hurt, resentment, or healing. In the free flow of the anus energy of apana, nothing can get to you, as there is no "you" to be got at, as you hold onto nothing.

The anus reveals where you lack knowledge concerning yourself and your deeper creative pathways. It masks dishonesty about yourself, and holds a vision of the self that is filled with fear of reality. It holds where we are unloving to self, and unaware of a need for change. When the anus opens and is healed, an opening of the pathway for needed positive change can occur.

Anus healing can reveal our deep need for change; it allows the surfacing and transmutation of hidden sadness and disease into light. It activates the earth-star chakra, and is part of the five-pointed root chakra circuit of spinal base, anus, perineum, yoni/lingam, clitoris/tip of lingam. As this important point activates, it leads us to be honest with ourselves, which leads to more self-love and satisfaction, and allows us to take charge and put change into action.

The anus carves a pathway through the shadow self. It allows polarities to be known, and it allows Shakti to flow in its full, unbounded state, without limits, without mind. Shakti—free of the control of mind, free to move and create spontaneously, creatively, and organically in each and every moment, unbridled by conventional restraints and cultural rigidities—is what led so many women to be persecuted and killed in the past, burnt as witches or heretics by churches and tribes that were scared of a power they did not understand, and could not control. Now it is up to you to reclaim your power by venturing into these areas, by venturing into their shadow, and using the power held there to create more beauty, empowerment, and love.

☙ Anus Breathing

You can reclaim the power of your shadow side by contacting the flow of apana. One way in which we can begin to move this stagnant, stuck energy is through *mudra* and breath. Mudras are specific hand gestures that connect into the body's organs and acupuncture meridians, stimulating them in order to awaken, vitalize, and clear these electrical pathways. The Apana Mudra supports our efforts to let go, allowing our fears to flow through, and out, from us.

The Apana or Anus Mudra

1. On both hands, bring your middle and ring fingers together with your thumb.
2. Focus on your anus and your breath, contracting and expanding the anus in time with your breaths. If you wish to accelerate the process, you can do fast breathing and fast contractions.

3. Now visualize a shameful, fearful, or guilty memory in your life.

4. With each inhalation, deep from the belly and anus, breathe in white light.

5. On the exhalation, breathe out black smoke from your anus. As you exhale this negativity out, feel the image or emotion you wish to let go of; release the old and unwanted debris of your life, be it physical, emotional, or mental.

6. Additionally, with each exhalation, you can sound the following mantra, letting the sound current flow down into your anus:

*OM PHNG**

Repeat for 10 minutes. Then rest and feel a new energy flow—the flow of apana.

I was taken into the deep cyclical nature of the anal breath. I was surprised in asking for the revealing of the deepest thing I am holding onto to have an immediate knowing—pride. As the breath continued, there were sensation points in my throat and back right side of the brain. At one point, I was sensing so much vibration and fire in the center of my brain that I wondered if I was doing it wrong.

With the intent to unveil the deepest fear or need that my ego continues to hold, I surrendered, allowing the anus breathing to create the ground in which to view, with brutal honesty, that which I am holding, that which runs my mind and controls my thoughts, words, and actions: the need for love and understanding, the need to be seen in the "goodness" of my being, the need to control the depth of my sexual power, the need to control the creative flow, to measure it out in small, unnoticed ways. (C.O.)

And within this I feel the need born from the fear: a soft pleading voice. The desire to be embraced—unconditionally—in love and wholeness. The

---

*PHNG is pronounced FNG as in PHarmacy.

body has its own wisdom. And to see this need for what it is, to embrace my Self with this soft compassion. To wholly extend the acceptance, the love, and the sweetness. And to hold myself in this space is my doorway to once again trusting MYSELF . . . and to melting the fear and the pulling away from power. These things must be met with embrace, not force. (A.T.)

With every release of the anus, my pulsing deepens . . . . I view, with compassion and resolve, the "shit" that is moving through: people, relationships, needs, wants, comforts, fears, and expectations. Emptying the files, the memory banks that block the flow, allows the breath to stir the living waters of this body, and excrete the sludge that binds me. (M.R.)

I began to have thoughts and feelings of deep appreciation for my anus; very surprising, loving feelings . . . deeper and deeper. The anus was no longer an outcast; labelings of dirty/stinky were dissolved. My anus was no longer exiled in separation as less godly than any other part of me. Feelings of love and beauty were swirling throughout my being.

My being as anus included feelings of deeper gratitude and compassion for the role it had taken on as the holder/the keeper/the guardian of things/circumstances that I was unequipped to process at the time they occurred. The anus responded by saying "If I am ready to take a look at these things now, with the intent of transformation, then they need to be dealt with system-wide." The anus is no longer willing to hold itself in separation as outcast, as unworthy, unholy, or the only one to do the job. The anus refused to take the brunt of the shutting down of my whole self, and invited all of me to participate. (K.M.)

If the anus is the guardian or keeper of these blocked off aspects of self, then the womb is their transmuter. When awareness upon the breath is brought to the anus, shedding light on these things, the breath then can become the transport to bring them to the womb. Womb holds them in the vast darkness of her being—holding them there in loving compassion until their compact nature begins to be infused little by little with space—stretching the tightly held patterns ever further apart until at last they have no remaining structure or form. This is dissolution; part of the wombs alchemical nature: of creation and dissolution, and perfect balance. (T.A.)

CENTERING HEAVEN AND EARTH

To center our bodies, minds, and souls means that we live with our bodies in the flow of the soul. The soul's energies flow through the central channel of the spine, which holds all the stresses and tensions collected by the bodymind and soul over many lifetimes. All of these energies connect through the central channel and the perineum. The perineum is a soft area between the anus and genitals that acts as the entryway and exit point for your spinal energies. It is the site of many blood vessels and nerve endings, and is quite sensitive. As the stresses, wounds, and tensions accumulated here begin to dissolve, we gradually become lighter, less judgmental, more loving. To center ourselves means that we are living with our bodies in the flow of the soul.

The perineum is part of the root chakra, which generates and grounds all of the energy in the physical body. The perineum stands in the middle of our personal, sexual desires, holding them in balance and maintaining harmony with the top of the spine—the impersonal crown chakra and third eye, centers of light and intuition. The perineum holds these polarities together and unites them through the spinal flow. It enables us to experience the reality of sexual energy and light energy mixing and merging within us, to create one flow of living light.

The perineum grounds the spine through the central channel of the pranic tube, the conduit that runs through our spines from the top of the neck down into the earth, and then to the center of the earth. Like the spinal base, the central channel provides a platform, a solid foundation for the ascent and descent of energy along the spine. But whereas the spinal base works with denser energies, the central channel anchors more subtle energies, holding them in harmony and balance.

The central channel, or pranic tube, ensures that your spine is kept connected to all of your chakras. It anchors the middle way between male and female energies, providing the basis for unity and neutrality, where male and female dissolve into simply being—energy without polarity. When this tube is open, energy runs smoothly. When it's closed, energy becomes lopsided.

The perineum anchors the bodymind by grounding us into our human bodies with love. It holds us in place to allow the human and divine parts of the self to flow together as one. Many healers use central channel breathing exercises and the perineum to turn themselves into conduits for healing energies from Heaven and Earth, which can then be focused to benefit their clients.

♣ Central Channel Breathing

This is a simple but powerful Tibetan Tantric breathing practice designed to open the central channel of the nervous system. It also accelerates your mastery of the breath, and your conscious control of the bodymind's reactions and responses. This practice serves to take you deeper into stillness, into the witness consciousness, and toward the more refined qualities of soul light found in the center of the spinal column. It helps to open the third-eye chakra, and is also used in Tantric lovemaking to channel energy up the spine into the heart and brain.

1. Sit up comfortably, spine straight.
2. Focus your first two fingers on one of your hands and point them at your root chakra/perineum.
3. Focus on the thin white line of light that runs through the center of your spine.
4. Purse your lips as though you were going to blow out a candle.
5. In this position, inhale light up the front of your body for 7 seconds, using your fingers to direct the energy of breath and light upward.

6. At the count of 7, cross your eyes gently and raise them to the third eye.
7. Hold your breath at the third eye for 7 seconds.
8. Exhale down the spine for 7 seconds, using your fingers to guide the energy.

Repeat the whole process 12 times. How do you feel afterward?

In doing this practice, some people experience orgasmic feelings, some people see colors and lights, some people feel the flow of light, and others feel deep peace, centeredness, and clarity. Many blocks can also arise as you do this breathing, showing you where your spine and chakras are blocked. By practicing, you can dissolve these blocks. You can also increase the breathing count to 12/12/12, and more, when you are ready.

It is best to do this practice in the morning to take the feeling into your whole day. When you do, how is your day different?

The Seven Gates to the Grail Womb

Timeless Pathway to Feminine Truth

THE SEVEN GATES HOLD A key for a woman to become fully embodied in her divine feminine nature. These seven gateways hold a powerful, timeless pathway to feminine truth, a pathway that has been forgotten and is now being remembered again, for the seven gates are a key to embodying the Grail within.

The seven gates were originally known and practiced by the Priestesses of Isis, and were used to empower and guide women into experiencing and using their full Shakti through the crucible of the womb. This then enabled them to empower men into the divine masculine, to initiate men into many aspects of life, from lovemaking, sacred union, and birthing to co-creation and the balance between male and female. To initiate a man into this spaciousness and Presence required that he enter a fully open womb through these seven gates.

The womb is the crucible of creation. Each woman holds this loving power to create and manifest from her own womb, which becomes the portal to the Cosmic Womb from which all creation springs, and into which all dissolves back. The womb is one of the last great mysteries to be revealed in this age, although it has been known and used in the past in cultures such as the Mayan, Tibetan, Indian, Gnostic Christian, and Egyptian among others.

The seven gates are a set of energetic portals that open the Way into the womb. They form a channel from the yoni to the G-spot, or Gratitude Spot, to the clitoris, moving through the cervix into the womb and the fifth, sixth, and seventh gates—the spaciousness of the Cosmic Womb. When healed, nourished, remembered, and honored as sacred, these seven gates become a royal road into the Grail of the Womb: they become the keys to manifestation of the divine feminine. Keys to Creation itself. Each gate opens as you progressively heal each part of the yoni and womb, making them sacred portals once again. As each gate opens, one by one, the level of openness and ability to experience love and overflowing embrace and surrender also deepens. This deepening occurs in direct relationship to what you are able to let *in*, to the extent that you are able to be physically, emotionally, and spiritually vulnerable.

The palpable Presence of these gates has been forgotten, lost within. The power of woman that you hold deep within her body is right here; all you need is a gentle reminder, a loving touch, to begin the process of making sacred what you already have innately within you. You are perfect as you are; now is the time to remember that. With gentle focus on each gate, touching it with your breath, feel the sparking of life force at each threshold. Love and bathe each gate with conscious Presence, igniting and firing its reawakening, and true purpose.

Touching the Lips of Love—the first gate at the threshold of the yoni—massaging them into fullness, opens the pathway to the second gate. This gate, known as the G-spot or gratitude spot, is wreathed in streaming waterfalls, cascading through every cell of your body. Bathed in love, its sensuality amplifies and readies you for the third gate, the blooming red rose of the clitoris, velvet to the touch, the pleasure of true love and the deep sensitivity to loving, and being loved.

This rose leads you to surrender to the river flowing to the fourth gate, the cervix, the portal to the womb, a star gate, a sacred diamond opening. Crossing through this portal into the vastness of womb, you

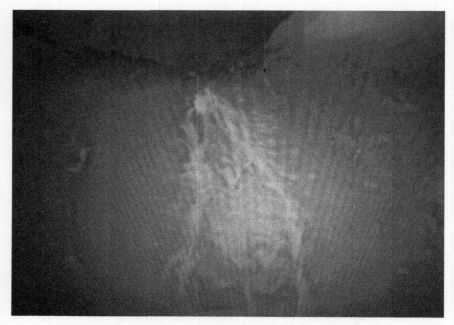

The second gate is wreathed in streaming waterfalls of love.

can feel the peace and remember. In that knowing, journey through gates five, six and seven, through the great central sun to the source of being: the Grail within. It is a memory within every cell of your being.

The seven gates stir memories of the power that manifests within. Integration of these memories is a key to opening and crossing each threshold. Allowing yourself to be penetrated by a male consciousness is the key to opening *all* of the gates *if* you are in a physical relationship. However, many female mystics have opened some of the gates through surrendering to God in a personal form, such as a lover of Krishna (a gopi) would, or like female Christian mystics who asked for, and were penetrated by, the Holy Spirit. However, in today's world of interconnection and the embodiment that only an intimate physical relationship can provide, the main way to access this is through committed relating between man and woman.

The inviting of the masculine essence to come deep into you requires that you become totally vulnerable, opening, embracing, surrendering to, and receiving the male essence in its totality. How deeply do you trust the masculine? When the seven gates are open, you are letting a man deep into your soul and your feminine essence, fully into the womb consciousness, which also has enormous benefits for him.

This letting in, of course, can only happen through deep mutual intimacy and surrender to the other. When enough sexual, emotional, and heart healing has been done by both partners—both alone and in the mirror of relationship—then this penetration and surrender can occur, organically unfolding the gates. The level of mutual love, trust, commitment, and willingness to grow are key factors in this, as well as the ability of the man to be able to support the woman, to be the safe pillar for the woman, therefore letting her go deeper into her own essential feminine nature and deeper into the womb consciousness, taking the masculine with her.

The gates begin with the first gate at the opening of the yoni lips and progress into the seventh gate of the fully open womb. The gates become more like energetic veils of emotion and love when one reaches the fourth gate and beyond, which is the opening into the womb of pure space and infinite potential. At this point, you start to access the subtler energies of the womb and of the unmanifest.

One starts to make love in a different way on the subtle planes and goes deeper into bliss. The man becomes swallowed in the infinite womb and surrenders to this drawing inward into the depths where all men wish to go, back to the source of life, and original innocence. The man becomes humbled and empowered in a new manner and the woman rests in ease and deep acknowledgment of her own divine nature, born from the deeper connecting and opening of the womb and heart. Divine Feminine and Divine Masculine are born.

THE TWO RIVERS

A woman can strengthen her individuality when she removes her essential feminine self from the existing social values, family structures, cultural conditionings, and expectations. In separating herself momentarily from the masculine—traditionally done in sacred traditions for a thirteen-day cycle with this intent—she finds her roots in her feminine nature, enabling her to become fully Self contained, empowered, and connected. She finds a foundation in the roots of the Eternal Feminine within her own inner divinity. She accesses a deeper strength, insight, intuition, and her own individual center. This also has deep implications and healing for the man in her life.

This individuality is found and realized by exploring the two rivers flowing through either side of the yoni itself: the dark river and the white river. The free-flow of Shakti brings up the dark river, the Black Goddess of lust, repression, and fear—the bad girl—revealing it, reveling in it, and expressing it until it finds its civilized form, an expression of power and authority centered in Self. Shakti also serves to reveal the ideas of the white river, the ideal of the perfect woman—the good girl—here to do the things expected of her by others. She is pure, holy, a perfect mother, lover, and partner.*

The true essence of Shakti balances both the dark and light: the two rivers flow through each side of the yoni up into the fourth gate, where the guardians of each river then unite in the opening of the womb.

In this journey, we find that the black river can ignite, reveal, transform, and inspire us. In the past, this dark river was condemned for its power to enflame women into free expression and embodiment of their sexual power. Many witches were burnt for knowing and consciously using this power to create with, and many more women were hung during the Inquisitions for embodying this power.

The white river of purity, holiness, order—the ideal of a civilized woman in her right place—has for many centuries been the accepted cultural norm for what a woman should be. This ideal describes a nice, sweet, loving person without the power to transform herself profoundly, some-

---

*Please take note: If you have a mother fixation and feel that you should receive unconditional love from your partner or anyone at all, you are unable to express and feel love fully with your present partner and are hiding deep guilt and wounding.

The white and dark rivers

one incapable of challenging or confronting things beyond the economic or cultural surface, a woman who knows her place in a man's world.

It is fear of the power of the black river that keeps women in the role of the white goddess—running away from full empowerment and full potential. In the times we live in, this form of behavior has run its course, for the black river brings up the deepest darkness, the most powerful wounds you have, and in so doing enables you to reclaim your power fully. The black river fuels both power and love in an embodied, visceral manner.

Shakti brings us what we need in order to grow. Shakti fulfills the desires of those who are pure, by giving rise to the actions necessary for their fulfillment. These actions, sometimes pleasant, sometimes not, lead us to a state of being in which we remember that in giving, we receive. Shakti leads to the deepest fulfillment, where all paths begin and end.

By having distorted, culturally created ideals of what women or men should be, we confine Shakti to a heavenly, "out there" state of idealized being that hides, and will eventually reveal, a demonized state. That which is unattainable is by nature incomplete, and ultimately inhuman. The Church's version of the Virgin Mary as a holy saint without sexuality, and of Mary Magdalene as a prostitute are perfect examples of this idealization, of the two rivers. Shakti brings us into our humanity fully, into our bodies fully, into relationship with all parts of ourselves fully.

All voices within our many-layered selves can be heard and expressed, felt and connected to through the free flow of Shakti. Bringing the lusty engagement for life of the Black River, and the love, purity, and serenity of the White River together heals the split in our femininity and masculinity. By expressing both, we can unite both in passionate, joyful, and loving embrace.

Magdalene is best known today for embodying the "pure" Divine Feminine, yet she is also cast as a dark, helpless, insignificant prostitute; two different views, both of which have some truth to them. This is because the Grail forms within us by uniting the pure white and lusty dark rivers of Shakti. These rivers of life force flow through each woman, creating and dissolving life.

The white river and the dark river are the sources of liking and disliking, attachment and aversion, pushing and pulling. These forces act on the mind each and every day, taking us away from our center of balance and equanimity. The white river impels us to like virtues, to be attracted to them, and to dislike that which we consider to be evil, negative, or bad for us—the dark river.

When we consider that what is good for us today may be bad for us tomorrow, and what is bad for us today may be the most beneficial thing for us tomorrow, we realize that staying attached to this ideal of righteousness actually makes us rigid. This type of thinking is what creates religions, leading to various forms of dogma and control, the most extreme being the Christian Inquisition, where thousands were massacred in the name of Christ.

Righteousness, or the desire for light to the exclusion of all else, leads to rejection of our own darkness, and of lessons we might learn from matter and the subconscious. This misplaced rigidity has led to some of the greatest wars on our planet, and the false notions of some religions being "better" than others. Love includes all in its embrace, regardless of what we are.

The Dark River influences our mind in the opposite way. Our mind is constantly tossed between these two spiraling forces of manifestation, forcing us to remain caught in the maelstrom of our likes, dislikes, attachments, and aversions—what we think is right or wrong.

As my life had been focused in the river of light, there was not an awareness of the beauty and power of the dark river flowing just below the surface. It was only thought of or felt as the place of despair, grief, sadness, pain, and suffering. And it can grab hold, drowning you in those frequencies, and veil the well-kept secret and magic of its power to transmute and create. The discovery of the dark river, and merging it with the river of light in sacred marriage, opens one to the full and never-ending flow of Shakti in a pure and powerful way. (C.O.)

The White River of Holy Desire: The Opener of the Way

Appreciation and gratitude are the openers of the white river, whose flow can be best called holy desire. When appreciation and gratitude are felt in the yoni, it becomes a holy portal to the universal womb. Flowing from the heart, appreciation and praise heal the yoni in a sanctified atmosphere, preparing the womb for sacred union that heals and blesses the man as much as it does the woman.

These upward spiraling emotions of appreciation, gratitude, love, and compassion are natural feelings that form the basis of union. When they flow into your yoni from your sacred heart—or from your partner's heart—healing of old wounds can occur.

Holy desire is sexuality raised to a level of unconditional love and giving. Not just in lovemaking, but in the desire for the Divine in all parts of your life and relationships. Through this complete vulnerability you find yourself as love begins to master you. We give in order to give, not give in order to receive.

Holy desire is a wanting, an inner burning that propels you, fuels you to keep moving forward. Holy desire is passion to fulfill the soul's deepest yearning, passion to be all that you can be. Holy desire makes us give our all. Desire is the energy that makes all things grow, flower, and bloom. It enables the soul to expand and reach for the infinite, and to surrender to the infinite, despite the fears that may arise. Holy desire never ends, as the universe is always expanding, as is the soul. The soul's desire for love can never be completely fulfilled. It is ongoing.

Holy desire is the beating heart of the soul; it is the life force of the soul, the soul's blood. Without this blood flowing through the soul's veins, we are lifeless, hollow. When the flow of desire is blocked, we start to die. When we forget our passions and allow them to fall by the wayside, then we lose a part of ourselves. The death of desire is the death of the soul, a death that only a profound shake-up can then reignite.

No matter how enlightened we become there is always more. In wanting more and stating it, we let God know that we want Her. It is important to want God. Tell Her so, every day. Holy desire is the life force, the golden thread that connects you and God. The more you amplify the voltage going through this thread, the more God will sit up and take notice, and actually send you more.

Holy desire can be an intense force—sensual, powerful, and overwhelming. This is why many fear it; because once it is released you will not be able to control it, as it leads to the overflowing of the life force in you. When we live in holy desire we cannot be controlled, for we flow in life itself. We can, however, choose when to allow the tap of desire to be open, what effects and manifestations it will have, and how we choose to act on any wave of desire flowing through us.

Desire grows through intimacy, intimacy grows through desire. The more intimate we become with each other, the more we desire and want to know more, and have more.

Be intimate with God; desire God. Redirect your desires towards this. Want God like a lover, deep inside you. Make love with God in this dance; show God your desire to be possessed by Him or Her. Always want more of God; let this be your prayer every day.

The Black River Speaks

I am your exhaustion, the heaviness, the fatigue of matter dragging you down. I am the entryway into the blackness, pulling you down deep, spiraling inward. I am the weight of matter, pulling you into form, into embodiment. I am the opposite of light, yet we work together to bring you into the here and now.

I am your resistance, the screams and cries of terror, the tears that have bound you into being a slave of the body. I am your sighs, the tiredness that overwhelms you, that keeps you inert. I am the grief and sorrow that keeps you stuck in your patterns. I am the body weighing your soul down, grinding you down until you sit and recognize me and my power. I am the energy within all matter, encoded within your bones, waiting to become crystalline by your surrender into my deep, dark well.

Sink into me. Fall down and spiral deep, losing your consciousness, gaining your freedom. Surrender to my embrace, the hug of matter, as we again become united.

Let your light descend. Enter the body; I will hold you and bring you real life. Allow yourself to become the heaviest you have ever been, and I will make you light again. I am the memory of the body, I am the memory held within the body, I am the memory that leads to your true Self once you have embraced and woven me into your life.

I am sloth, I am inertia; I am gravity, I am stability. I am your body. I make you solid and tangible. I am the sleep that hides within you until you contact me.

I am the perfect stability that supports Creation into being. I am the fluid silence of physical mastery. I am the glue of matter that binds atoms together. I am bondage, suffering, death, and inertia that you are too scared to face and acknowledge. I am part of life, and I signal the beginnings of new life. Enter death and you enter life.

I am the voice of your resentments, your loneliness, your feelings you have rationalized spiritually and intellectually. I am the voice that hides underneath your spiritual and political correctness. I am the root of your irritation with yourself.

I am the emptiness of your humanity, and I show you where you have betrayed your humanity. I am that which you have to dare to express, to take courage to share. I am the voice lurking in the shadows, waiting, festering, for a moment to speak. I remind you of your glamorizations. I remind you of the human truth of relationship, not the white truth, but the grounded truth.

I show you your illusions and your fantasies that you design to keep you safe at night. I show you the falsity of your Presence, and what lies underneath it. I show you the real you, warts and all. I show you what you do not wish to see.

So honor me. Honor my voice within you. Keep the balance between your human needs and your divine giving. I ground your selflessness onto Earth, into the body. Honor your bodyworld and its impulses. Do not let me take over, for if I do I will lead you into the deepest slumber and forgetting. I am the voice of matter trapped in light, and when honored I am the voice of Shakti released. I am the voice of the primal web of life, here and now relating on Earth.

So speak my name: scream it, whisper it, growl it, sing it. Love it all. My voice is your truth. Let me slip through your lips, just a droplet—a sigh, a soft moan—and flow with it, allow it, follow it back to my source. In this way you become the river. Breathe into whatever darkness arises, and breathe it out into expression. I am unearthing your shadow. All your griefs, joys, primal rage—what are they all but flow? Soft eddies and vast waters, all of it is love. (W.C.)

When trapped in my embrace, you become steeped in ignorance, not even
aware of my existence. You just go on fulfilling the mundane obligations of
life, caught in their descending cycle, caught in a matrix. (P.A.)

BEGINNING THE JOURNEY

Great pathways of pain lie carved in the bodies of women, ages and
ages of collective suffering are pressing closed the doorways to your own
liberation. In forgetting the legacy of women's power, you have suffered
the pain of being separated from parts of yourself you are no longer
taught to honor, and whose wisdom you no longer heed. The power is
within you, and you are being called now to find and reclaim your inner
divinity. To do this, you must first go into the darkness, discover all the
ways you have repressed yourself and have been repressed, all the ways
in which you have abandoned and forgotten your true nature. It is all
stored in your body.

Your journey through the seven gates will take you into that darkness, and will bring you back out into a clearer light. This is the gift
that awaits: your greatest pain, and your greatest freedom. Each of these
gates has a voice to express. Each has its own nature and expression and
each carries the pain and weight of having been separated from its own
divinity.

Experiencing praise and pleasure, intertwined with ignorance, disrespect,
mutilation, and pain at the first gate, entrance to the yoni, brought me into
a deeper presence and appreciation with the "lips of love." The pulsing of
the G-spot sent me swirling into the maelstrom of rape, violence, abuse,
and misuse, with only a momentary memory of any acknowledgment or
gratitude being expressed to me in the past. In the first touch of the third
gate, the clitoris, the black rose in the dark river, a shiver of pleasure made
way for the horror and pain of mutilation, molestation, and the numbness
there that remains.

Yet I am re-membering. A raging river of darkness, hidden below the

goodness, the peace, the beauty. My power, my fury, is not to be tempered.
I will burn away all resistance, all hesitancy, and all memory that wants to
control my flow. It is time. (C.O.)

The journey requires you to unite the light and dark rivers of Shakti.
This deeply loving practice of opening the gates is an integral part of
clearing the eighteen pathways. This culminates in the Shakti Circuit,
which gathers all the energy to flow up the spine from the womb,
through to the yoni, the perineum, the anus, the base of the spine, and
then up through the interweaving currents of the spinal column into
the Mouth of the Goddess.

In a woman's body, Shakti comes to life as the river of light emanating
from the wellspring at the seventh gate deep within the womb. This river
connects the womb to her true journey and sets her on the path that is the
ever-spiraling flow of giving and receiving. So it manifests through women
and men in a constant state of service, of giving in every moment, the giving
that is simply being totally present and sharing of the Shakti flow out in
every direction.

So, women, by being able to access Shakti directly, find that in receiving
from the Source, they in turn are led to give. Men, however, access Shakti
through the woman's form by first giving. Do you see the divine dance
displaying itself once again? The woman in receiving, gives, the man in
giving, receives. Only by reaching a place of conscious awareness to lead
himself to the fifth gate in union with a woman will he access the true levels
of Shakti that lie beyond it. In order to even access the fifth gate with a
woman, his journey will already be one of openness, clarity, self-awareness,
and giving. In giving, so he receives, and when they join in the deepest union
at the fifth gate he can then journey with her to the sixth and seventh gates
to experience the eternal well-spring that is held within her. (T.A.)

The First Three Gates

Lips of Love, the Gratitude Spot, and the Blooming Red Rose of the Clitoris

THE LABIA, THE LIPS OF love, form the entrance to the yoni. They are guardians not just of the body, but also of soul. They are the flowering sentinels who serve your sacred well and life force, and whose message is "I honor myself." The second gate, the G-spot is the gate of gratitude. It is a fountain of ecstatic, erotic pleasure that gives both partners the gift of a woman's arousal. The red rose, a symbol of the Grail and of Magdalene, is the third gate: the clitoris. The third gate opens only in the bliss and purity of love.

THE FIRST GATE: THE LIPS OF LOVE

One enters the first gate with praise and appreciation. Praise begins to heal you of your own subjective, or inner, experience of life. It is a foundation for love, as appreciation leads to true gratitude and the ability to see the beauty in all beings. Praise, the gatekeeper of the first gate, allows us to let go of limiting habits of self-judgment and condemnation, and awakens us to the beauty and divinity of others, and ourselves.

As the first gate is cherished, she adorns you. When in her essence, she throbs with fragrance and her full lips bloom, sweet and inviting. To receive the fullness of her hidden gifts, pause and reflect. The more reverence and gratitude you present, the sweeter the gifts you will receive in return. In approaching the yoni with a sense of being honored by a great presence, rather than being out to "get" something, you open into infinite possibilities of experience and rapture.

Praise brings you into the beauty and divinity of another, and of your Self. Honoring and appreciating are the basis for kindness and gratitude, the basis for love. Without praising, without appreciating, we shrink and wilt into our ego, allowing it to be the master with the soul as servant. Vulnerability and humility open the doorway to love and intimacy. Without vulnerability and humility, appreciation and devotion, the gates can never fully open, and the Grail womb cannot be entered. In giving these qualities, we receive them.

The first gate opens us into trust. For women, this trust is about surrendering to your own nature—to the soft, open, receptivity of your being. Trust yourself, and what it is you are letting in, or keeping out. The wounds women carry here, both personal and collective, revolve around this issue of trust. For men to come fully into this first gate they must approach it with both praise and purity, fully honoring this sacred portal into the feminine.

For a woman to surrender into this space of trust she must respect her own sanctity and feel respect and praise from the man she is with. The nature of relationship today has led to a deep forgetting of this sacred path, and most women hold a great unconscious sadness at the loss of their connection to the Divine Feminine, which is accessed through this first gate. And with it, the loss of the profound sense of communion and wholeness that comes from fully honoring, and being honored by, your partner.

True praise and appreciation allows the small self to fall away. It is this small self's fear that in praise it will be giving away its power, love, and beauty to something outside itself. There is nothing outside itself. In praise you feel the beauty, vision, and perfection of another welling up inside yourself, and speak it—to honor the very gift and wonder of that person's existence . . . of all existence. To see, feel, and honor another's presence fully, whether human or Divine, allows the gift you perceive in another into your own heart, body, and soul. In fully giving your appreciation to another you feel the depth to which he or she is always and only a reflection of your self.

To be devoted means to be committed to giving to your partner, to your soul purpose, to your healing, and to God. These qualities enable all the gates to open and flower. Devotion is serving the flowering of love, allied with the appreciation of another's efforts, struggles, or endeavors that can give that person the impetus to continue, persist, push on, especially when he or she struggles to do so. So devotion is gratitude—for something that touches you emotionally, for someone else's struggles or efforts, for the wonderful gifts of life that creation surrounds us with.

Prostration: Making You and Your Partner Sacred

A beautiful way to deeply appreciate and praise each other is through prostration. In prostrating yourself to the God in your partner before you make love, you refine and recognize the powerful energy of desire as sacred, and honorable. Prostration brings the experience of surrender and union to both of you. It is the end of pride, ego, and attachment, and the redirecting of raw desire into holy desire. When this happens, the Divine reveals itself.

In giving yourself to the other in prostration, you are giving yourself to the core of existence—to the Self. In this spirit, prostrations to your partner are the most selfish act you can perform. Nothing is more selfish, and yet nothing so purifies selfishness into selflessness: the secret is that you and your partner share the same Self.

Physically, prostrations open up the solar plexus chakra, our center of empowerment and selfless power, making us humble to the Divine in the other, and our own Self. You use your body as the vehicle for this recognition and acceptance of your own divine nature.

In prostration, communion occurs between soul and soul, lightbody and lightbody. Both partners share a common spirit and deepen their trust in each other. Here purity is the secret of fulfilling your desires. These desires come true when they are held in the heart.

To prostrate before your man is to prostrate before the Divine Man.

To prostrate before your woman is to prostrate before the Divine Woman.

♣ Prostrating to the Divine Within

Most relationships are based on need: you need your partner in order to become whole in some way. In this practice, we start to own the qualities we find attractive in the other, that we want to learn from the other, that we are missing in our own self. We fill the need by giving and recognizing. In prostration these qualities can be freely shared between partners. You prostrate to the qualities that you find appealing and attractive in the other—what the other represents to you on the deepest levels, both spiritually and emotionally. Which part of him or her fills the hole in you? In this, you can start to become what the other represents to you, and what you need from the other to become whole within your own self.

1. Identify three soul and emotional qualities that are attractive in your partner, and that you wish to embody within yourself. Share them with your partner. Decide between you that you will become them.

2. Hold one quality in mind. Stand silently in a sacred heart space in front of your partner, and place your hands in prayer pose above your head. You are treating your partner as a living God, so sink into this space. Imagine you are in the Creator's Presence. How would you treat this Presence?

   Your partner is holding the energy of the quality you are prostrating to. For example, if you value and need your partner's sense of gentleness and empathy, she will be holding that energy for you as you stand before her, and prostrate before her. She can take any body position—sitting, standing, holding a mudra, or her arms and legs in whatever position most embodies gentleness.

3. Now place your hands above your heart. Sink to your knees, and place your body flat on the ground, with your hands stretched out in front of you, head on the ground. Feel your heart on the earth. Breathe and draw gentleness into yourself. The partner who is upright transmits those qualities to the partner who needs them.

Now reverse the process for Partner A and B.
End each cycle of prostrations with a deep heart bow to each other.

> *Desire liberates if we follow it all the way to its source;*
> *Love.*
> *Desire liberates if we no longer separate or judge any part*
> *of ourselves.*
> *Desire liberates when we align it to its original purpose*
> *and choice: surrender to Life itself.*
>
> *May love's desires bless you.*
> *We are all Beloveds in our holy desire for union.*

The First Gate of the Black River

A growing number of women seem to hate the appearance of their vulvas, the first gate. Many women, some as young as fourteen, are worried that their genitalia is somehow disfigured or malformed. Much of this is due to miseducation, with the lack of any real guidance on how to be a woman, what a woman is, and how we are all different. Just as each lingam is different from all others, so is each yoni different from all others.

Adding to their self-doubt, many women are subject to comments from boyfriends who have not stepped into their true masculinity; such comments play on girls' deep insecurity about their womanhood. With no role models, and secular families having no interest in what lies behind the appearance, women are increasingly becoming educated by the media on what a woman is, or should be.

The shame surrounding the first gate or the lips of the vagina/yoni is reaching epidemic proportions in modern day culture. Vaginal cosmetic surgery has doubled in the UK over the past five years, and in the private sector there has been a 300 percent increase in labiplastys, making it the fastest growing form of cosmetic surgery in the UK. This surgery simply makes the yoni "look" a certain way. It is purely aesthetic, and does not accentuate pleasure; it is designed solely to make the yoni appear attractive according to modern definitions of what attractive is, defined in this case by men.

In Europe, metal chastity belts were clipped around the vagina, to keep it "pure" for the husband's private use. Of course many diseases and infections arose from this practice. Vaginal surgery was done in primitive cultures to control women, to keep them in their place. In Africa, clitoral and vaginal cutting are still commonplace; ritual surgeries are designed to stop women from having pleasure so they will stay with their husbands.

The modern "choice" to have vaginal surgery goes back to the same psycho-sexual roots: shame, and a lack of love for the sacred space of the lips of the yoni. This deep wound allies with the need to keep up with the pressures of modern day consumer society, where sex sells almost everything, including the idea of love.

Just as breast implants and tummy tucks are now commonplace, so is clitoral and hymen stitching, with vagina alteration becoming the next fad. In 2008 a poll on UK TV's Channel 4 reported that over 42 percent (3375 votes) of women polled said yes, they had considered having vaginal surgery to enhance the look of their vaginas.

Underlying all of this is the ignorance that surrounds the vagina and true sensuality. This ignorance, fostered by a lack of open discussion, is a breeding ground for insecurity and self-judgment, self-loathing, and fear. The vagina is the passage inside, and the word literally means "somewhere to sheathe your sword." Even the word means a woman's sexual organs exist only in relation to men.

The word *yoni,* from Sanskrit, is a far more appropriate term for this sacred space from which all life emerges. It means the divine passage, the holder, the matrix of generation, the origin or primal source of all being, the birthplace of the universe. Each child is considered to be born from a yoni of stars—constellations that prevailed during the child's birth.

The yoni or first gate is a temple where the divine essence of a woman can be connected with and worshipped. It is the gateway to the infinite, which rises through six other gates into the womb, the birth space for all life. It is where a woman learns true self-love and self-respect by only allowing in that which is loving and honoring of her essence.

Healing the First Gate

A common practice for starting to heal the first gate is called yoni gazing. This requires a sacred intent on behalf of both partners to be vulnerable, open, and honest with their feelings.

♣ Yoni Gazing

1. To begin this practice, the sacred woman lies down and spreads her legs.
2. The sacred man lies between her legs, and looks at her yoni intently, with relaxed focus. This can quickly take the man into an alpha state of meditation, and bring the woman into different feelings of insecurity and shame, and eventually peace and healing. The urge to giggle may arise, which is fine, as it provides a release of energy hidden behind embarrassment and shame. Just do not use it as an excuse to stop going deeper.

   Remember to keep breathing and allow the process. This practice is remarkably healing and insightful for men as well as women; it enables them to honor the feminine and also to

hear all the judgments they have ever held about women's bodies. Just allow it all and do not forget to commune and express
your experience with each other after the practice is complete.
The yoni gazing can last for up to 45 minutes. If you treat it as a
sacred healing practice, it will become one.

A Sacred Doorway

The first gate is the sacred doorway into your most holy of places. Many
women have forgotten this, and have allowed energies to enter that do
not respect or honor them. In essence, these women have disrespected
themselves by allowing these energies in. We each have the power to
demand that those who enter within us do so with love and honor.

Many people find anger, pain, and mistrust stored in the first gate.
These emotions come from screams not expressed, from anger and
hatred toward men for their ignorance in putting women down. Here is
stored rage at the disrespect shown to children who have been molested,
those who have been sold into sex slavery and shut themselves off from
feeling any other emotion beyond this gate just to survive the pain. Here
is heard the cries of these children, "Where is my protector, where is my
dad, my mom?" Sadness and loss of trust from having been violated and
unable to protect oneself reside in this first gate.

What affects one woman affects all women in the web of life, and
it is only through feeling the emotions of the collective in the first
gate—the first gate of all women, that you can be healed of them.
As these emotions heal in you, the web of life becomes that much
brighter for all.

Entering a woman and "going for it" without respect for the yoni,
without foreplay—just shoving the penis in for the man's own pleasure and self-gratification—is where sex becomes violence, ownership,
conquering, and animal aggression. By these actions, women lose their
sense of beauty and sanctity, their sense of being cherished. Gradually
their feminine power begins to fade away. The sense of safety, trust,
and vulnerability recedes as numbness sets in. The lips become desen-

sitized to true intimacy, and many women have little or no feeling beyond this gate.

This gate thus holds great sadness—for the loss of sanctity, all the ways it has been violated and forgotten. When the gate and its attendant sorrows are cleared, a woman is able to fully trust her own being. She holds herself and her sexuality as sacred, and knows when to surrender, when to be open, and also when to exert discernment and create boundaries. She does not trust blindly—she respects and knows her own intuition, and does not give this power away. She is a woman who knows her own worth and grants entrance only to those who are deserving and appreciative.

THE SECOND GATE: THE GRATITUDE SPOT

It is said that gratitude is the attitude of enlightenment. Flowing naturally in the wake of praise, gratitude begins to counter the judgments we have around our relationship with our bodies, and with the world around us. As the judgments we hold in these areas dissolve, we reconnect with the world as it is, rather than the world as we want it to be.

When gratitude is showered into the G-spot, it opens. Then Shakti herself wells up with gratitude at being experienced in her fullness for the first time in eons. She beams with exuberance, ready to share her gifts and knowledge. In her gratitude, Shakti wants to pour outward in even greater amounts, knowing that as she gives, she receives.

Gratitude results in a desire to give constantly; the circular flow of giving and receiving builds upon itself, which allows a continuous outpouring of love to flow from the soul filled with Shakti. This is one of Shakti's secrets that she does not reveal immediately. She lets you explore and discover her intimately first, feeling your way through ancient yet familiar pathways. She shares energy; she heals; she clears. She builds trust and then she expands into her true essence, letting you fall into a river of bliss. In her gratitude for being

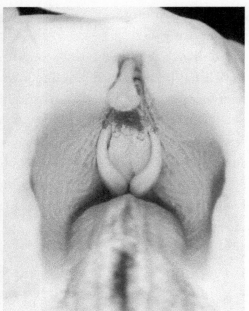

When gratitude is showered upon the G-spot, it opens just like a flower.

acknowledged, she lets you fall in love with her, and shows you your greatest potentials.

If you thank all things in your life, you gain a deeper understanding of your power as creator. You see that you truly have created everything that is happening to you, and that, in your magnificence, you have done so in order to learn ever-deeper lessons about compassion and love. This starts with your own love for yourself, and compassion for what you put yourself through in order to learn and remember.

If you bless all occurrences and people in your life, you spiritualize your whole experience, down to the most mundane events. Everything becomes an opportunity to grow into peace; everything becomes an opportunity to bring loving wisdom into your everyday life. The more you see this, the quicker you evolve and transmute any egoic resistance to the flow of gratitude.

For gratitude is the current of love that weaves its way throughout all life and all people. The more you thank the deeper lessons that darkness and fear present to you, the more you see their purpose, and the more humble you become to the beauty and divine orchestration of life as it is occurring to you now, in the present.

Gratitude flows in both the dark and light rivers; without it, there is neither true power nor the presence to create divinity. Kindness and gratitude are interlinked. In gratitude one realizes that you cannot *get* love, you can only receive it, and you can only fully receive it by giving it away. To have all, give all. To be truly happy is to live in gratitude. Living in gratitude and in grace means accepting whatever comes one's way, both good and bad, with thankfulness. There is no exception to what one can be thankful for, as gratitude wears down our resistance to conflicts, humbles us, and brings us into joy.

Try this: Thank all the painful and beautiful occurrences that happen to you today, and see how you feel. In the conflicts that arise, in the "unfortunate" circumstances that happen, there is a lesson that your soul has created in order to find the peace of an open, giving heart. This heart makes all things full by thanking them, and in the process empties itself of any resentment, frustration, or thoughts of harm.

This openness leads to beauty, which arises from the clarity of our own perception. Beauty is not about how a person, place, or object looks; it is about how you, who are looking, feel. The beauty that you experience "out there" is a direct reflection of the beauty that is happening inside you. When you are in a state of joy and feel uplifted, everything appears beautiful to you.

What we often describe as beautiful is an interpretation, a view that has been taught to us—a perception that one thing is beautiful, and another is ugly. To see beauty is to see with the heart, to see things as they are, and to appreciate them and connect with them in a heart-centered way. When we truly see reality it is beautiful, as it involves no judgment, no naming or identifying with things, no boxes or ideas, no past history of what we once felt was beautiful.

Without the mind's judgment and commentary, we can see the beauty in a rotting pile of dung lying on the street. If you have no judgment about the value of something, then you can appreciate the nature, and use, of all things. In true beauty we do not exclude anything, but embrace it all. Where we do not see beauty, we can see where our minds still judge and misunderstand. Heaven is not somewhere else; it is right here in this perception.

The Well of Darkness: The Second Gate of the Black River

The second gate is a great power generator of the yoni, and as such harbors rage at all the ways women have been disempowered, and have disempowered themselves. Women's collective memories of being repressed, tied up, shut up, shut down, raped, savaged—of playing small, of giving their power away to men, of feeling violated and impotent—all are seething and boiling here in the second gate.

The rage comes from feeling powerless at the hands of aggression, both blatant violence and all the passive acts of aggression that have become acceptable in our society. It also is something women direct at themselves for having silenced their own expression. This is the place where women have turned all these acts of sexual violence and unconsciousness against themselves, and have cut themselves off from their own bodies and their own sexuality.

The second gate is a well and pit of suffering in the collective consciousness, where rivers of rage and shame manifest. Imagine that every minute of every day somewhere in the world, there is a woman curled up in the fetal position, rocking herself into cathartic slumber. Having been raped, abused, or routinely taken for granted, she thinks it is her fault, and has cut herself off from herself and from everyone else. She withdraws from life, disengages from the life force, and suppresses her rage at her loss of power. She feels physically helpless to do anything, and her self-worth plummets.

Healing the Second Gate

The feelings of isolation generated by this black river can be healed only by connection to others—by the sweet balm of gratitude and pleasure gifted and shared. As we share our gratitude with others, we begin to feel loved and appreciated over time, and to build feelings of trust and safety.

THE THIRD GATE: THE BLOOMING RED ROSE OF THE CLITORIS

Compassion is the natural response to a life of appreciation and gratitude. As one's consciousness naturally expands, compassion replaces judgment, which can create experiences of unworthiness and dissatisfaction in many areas of life, including our relationships with others.

When a woman feels the spirit of devotion being lavished upon her, and upon all beings, she is in contact with the essence of the third gate and her red rose blossoms.

When the third gate of the clitoris is stimulated it creates waves of resonance that nourish the central nervous system, feeding our intuitive and psychic abilities. When clitoral stimulation is accompanied by gratitude and enjoyment, our bodies create more of these same qualities. As this occurs, nerves along the spine can recalibrate and retune. Old programs are deleted, and thought patterns are rewired, enabling us to witness and transcend many limits of the mind that have covered the blooming red rose.

As this gate heals, purity, innocence, and sensual pleasure arises to take us into a deeper embrace of those parts of ourselves that are lost and isolated. This embrace allows us to heal abuses and feelings of disconnection and numbness from our bodies and our sexuality. As we soften our armor, we soften what is rigid within—the protection and the disconnection, the pain and numbness felt at the clitoris—to allow ecstasy to reawaken and reconnect us.

Ahh, what sweetness there is in connection. I take such pleasure in closeness, in feeling another's tenderness. When open, I am your center of joy and excitement, transforming all things back into their purest nature.

I leap outward in joy, exuberance, and embrace. All life is beauty to me. When open, I am your own heart's compassion.

Treat me with greatest appreciation, and I will return you to your own first innocence. With this healing process and this great gift of appreciation you have shown me, you will find in the circle of giving and receiving my own gifts back to you. Like the full rose with all of its petals opening out to the sun, with all of my cells accessible to the atmosphere, I become more sensitive to all the energies passing over me; the slightest breeze, shift in the sunlight, or fall of mist upon my petals sends ripples to my core. The more you receive it, the more you give joy back to me, and I continue to heal and clear deep within my being. (A.T.)

The Black Rose: Third Gate of the Black River

My petals are filled with the tears of ignorance, of being touched, sucked, licked, bitten, and rubbed raw in the for-getting without the for-giving. Manipulated and stimulated without true presence, one will not know the velvet touch of my compassion, the sweet taste that is present in love's embrace. I am the rose, honoring the doorway to the Holy Grail, the eternal womb. Receive my folds in love and I am the spark . . . (C.O.)

Here lies the mutilation of clitoral cutting, and the shame of all the people involved in these ceremonies found in many religious cultures. Here is stored numbness, pain that leads to switching off in deep grief and sadness, knowing this is not the way it is supposed to be. Here is stored the clitoral shock at being touched inappropriately, incestuously or otherwise, and not knowing what to do with this feeling and its unexpressed emotions. Here lies the neglect and lack of appreciation of the clitoris.

Because our bodies intuitively know what is sacred, and what is not, we subconsciously protect ourselves from disrespectful and dishonoring stimulation and penetration. This protection can feel like heavy, thick energy sitting in our bodies, or in the space around us, manifesting as extra physical weight, as lethargy, as dullness of thought, or lack of motivation. A woman who feels physically violated may also disappear into her mind, "tuning out" and going numb in an attempt to avoid being present.

She is unable to describe her behavior as she is too used to this treatment. She knows no better and has been programmed over lifetimes to think this is normal. She lives in a man's world and is used to man's instant gratification with no depth of emotion or meaning. She may even fool herself into thinking that she is enjoying herself, finding sensory pleasure alone. The clitoris feels this suppression at the level of the soul. Women store this in their cellular memories and energetic patterning. These emotional veils build up over time and eventually crust over, until the clitoris is desensitized and disconnected.

Physical stimulation of the clitoris for titillating pleasure, rather than for love, only adds to the abuse of a holy yoni. Any person who watches a pornographic film knows how to physically stimulate a clitoris, but to devotedly love a clitoris is another matter that requires a good heart and purity of intention, a choice to have lust merge and refine into loving devotion.

Healing the Third Gate

When the clitoris is clear of wounds and misuse, it gives rise to feelings of innocence and sweet freshness, borne from gratitude, appreciation, and compassion. This gate can be worked on with a partner or in a retreat setting, where it can be felt into in a safe yet powerful way. It is hard to clear this gate without knowing what you are doing, and especially without going into both the light and dark rivers. However, the mystery of love between two committed people can heal this gate if both partners are truly open and aware.

When the first three gates are connected and healed both personally and collectively, the yoni becomes a portal to the Divine.

Being touched with praise, my lips quiver in rhythmic, pulsing breath. Gentle re-membering, feeling the honoring, the gratitude within the looping love flowing between us as my Second Gate is touched, receiving and giving in the pulsing breath of acknowledgment.

As the blooming rose of my Third Gate is touched by compassion, the breath of my being is felt in a soft presence on the surface. The river of fury, unleashed for moments earlier, is felt below the surface, molten lava that will not be controlled in its collapsing of the surface illusion of peace and harmony. To create anew, the old must be destroyed. True peace and harmony will arise within the balancing, the reharmonizing of our instruments. (C.O.)

You have to feel your own healing, and take on the collective healing, in order for the yoni channel to become a gateway into the infinite womb. This is the way it has always been done, and always will be done. What affects one woman affects all women in the web of life and interconnection that we all live in.

The Fourth Gate

Entering the Grail Womb

THE FOURTH GATE IS THE cervix, entrance to the holy of holies—the cosmic womb or Grail. Magdalene is known as the Grail for carrying the bloodline of Christ, yet she herself knew that the opening to the Grail lies through the fourth gate in each and every woman.

The fourth gate is a diamond doorway, a star gate: the opening into your womb is an opening into infinite space. This diamond shape is similar to the outer layer of the sacred geometrical figure known as the Sri Yantra (see diagram on page 14). The Sri Yantra is a pattern of the Goddess of all Creation, the creation that is held within the yoni and womb of all women.

❧ Traveling through the Fourth Gate

1. Visualize the diamond shape that is the opening in your cervix. Through this neck of your womb—the thick band of muscles that paves the way for new life to come into the world—you can also travel *toward* the womb, to the Grail within.
2. Bring your attention to your cervix, and try to isolate it, just focusing on that one area. Breathe here and ask yourself lovingly, "Can I feel this entry gate?"
3. If not, you may want to physically feel your cervix and allow your finger to just rest there. Bring breath and presence into it.

Now that you can feel it . . .

What do you feel here?

Do you see any colors, feel any sensations, emotions, do any memories arise?

What does she want to say to you?

What specifically does she want from you to open, and how can you best connect to her, and to your womb?

How does she want you to recognize and honor her?

Most neo-tantric sexual healing focuses on the personal healing only, neglecting the deeper, and larger picture of the collective feminine consciousness that must be experienced in order to turn the divine vessel of the yoni into the holy of holies: the Grail Womb. This means you travel through these arenas and cultivate a deeper empathy, a deeper compassion, a deeper opening within you that blesses and sanctifies your yoni for sacred union, and for the alchemy of co-creation that happens through the open yoni and womb. To have this open yoni, to enter the Grail Womb, means we travel into the darkest depths and the highest heights, with commitment, sincerity, and dedication to transmute what is held there.

THE DWELLER ON THE THRESHOLD

The fourth gate is known in alchemical terms as the Dweller on the Threshold. This is a vital place for all women to enter, and is the greatest barrier, and guardian, to the womb's mysteries. It is here that the reversal of roles happens: where the soul becomes master of the ego, instead of the ego being master of the soul. As the soul is made of love and giving, this is what you have to be living in order to enter union, in order to enter the womb. One has to be in a place of no need, and of giving, in order to open this gate; you have to be integrated and whole within yourself.

As the fourth gate opens, many voices of fear and resistance arise, for many issues are stored here on the most primordial levels. Here is where many of your deepest healings lie. It takes true courage, and deep vulnerability, to enter this gateway. You have to be prepared to let go of everything you do know, and have learnt, to enter this space. To be able to heal this with your partner takes true commitment, for it is the gateway to your deepest sadness, your deepest love, your most profound separation, and your most profound union between your inner male and female.

The fourth gate is a portal to many dimensions of experience: when you enter it, your life will change. For a man to enter this gate, a woman must trust him completely, surrender completely, and be totally vulnerable on a preverbal, primal level beyond words and thoughts. As he is allowed into the womb through the portals of appreciation, love, and trust, a man's consciousness enters pure space, and he feels the immense power of creation, as well as the power to create, accompanied by enormous loving bliss and the sheer beauty of love that is painful in its intensity. This has to be experienced to be believed; it is how sacred sexual union occurs between souls, not just between bodies and minds.

One can have glimpses of this opening into the fourth gate, but to integrate it is another matter. To integrate it means journeying to the fifth gate: unifying your inner male and female. This is a journey both within you and outside of you (in your outer relationships) and it requires all of you to participate; your sexual energy, your emotions, your body, your mind, and your soul all have to come together and express themselves in order to unify.

To be strong in sovereign Self-love is a key to entering the fifth gate. As a woman opens up even further from a place of strength, self-empowerment, autonomy, and independence, she can become more vulnerable, as now she understands this not as weakness but as strength. It is a feminine strength to be receptive and whole, and to allow your chosen man deep within you. This may take some time, as after the initial opening of the fourth gate, many healing issues arise in order to be integrated into self-empowerment.

For the fourth gate to open, you have to leave your comfort zones. The arts of Tantra and sacred relationship take on whole new dimensions, and become deeper and richer on many more levels of awareness. Indeed, the whole union of man and woman becomes possible through the opening of the seven gates, as the woman becomes open to the cosmic womb, drawing the man within this womb, which in turn dissolves them both.

The womb is the source of our greatest healing. Once we return to it, having healed all that happened on our journey away from it, we become whole.

THE VOICE OF THE WOMB

The womb first awakens as we bring her the gifts of Presence, devotion, deep respect, appreciation, and the feeling qualities of love and adoration. This begins the birthing phase. The womb will then begin to speak of her needs and desires. Only the purified heart will hear, only the courageous will respond.

The womb speaks the language of love. Nothing else will nurture and nourish her, or provide her the safety she needs to flower. She drinks in radiating light, the sweetness of silent conscious breath, and the sounds and vibration of harmony.

The womb does not understand the intellect and the ways of the world. She does not hear or respond to voices of fear or judgment. She will not expose herself to the impure, and she will not trust to bare her fruit for the foolish and ignorant. One must be prepared to take great risks and rise to challenges, and be tested in unexpected ways.

The jewel of an open womb is not for the meek and half-hearted. It is for the brave, and the strong-willed, for the heroes and heroines among you. For the womb to reveal herself, she needs to feel a genuine loyalty, and a love that surpasses all worldly desires. Only then can she begin to allow herself to be unveiled, and reveal the secrets of creation and the mysteries of life itself.

The womb's only desire is to feel the warmth of love and support from the feminine and masculine, which are both necessary for her to open and expand. The womb desires to attune to the masculine to feel his strength, protection, and love. The feminine must embody the womb in all its innocence and power, and the male must act according to her wisdom and guidance.

A deep love between inner man and inner woman creates a resonant vibration of sacred union where birth can be manifest in its fullest potential. When two unite and melt into the flames of love, the womb is ignited. All separate desires and individual agendas must be surrendered to the wisdom the womb holds. This is bringing Heaven to Earth, spirit into matter, love into form.

The womb is where the unmanifest is brought into manifestation—where beauty and joy are birthed into life as a juicy, orgasmic, tangible experience. When love is anchored into form, into reality, into a direct lived experience, only then shall the truth be known. Total respect and humility is offered for this voice to come forth. This voice is recognizable as a soft powerful clarity. It is the voice of the feminine—pure, gentle, and graceful, yet powerful, direct, and deep. It does not compromise or search for approval. It does not speak of duality nor does it muster words of fear and doubt. It remains calm and precise, knowing exactly what is required in each and every moment.

At this stage, the voice of the ego will likely emerge, fearful of its own death and trying to reassert control over the heart in order to stay alive. The ego has been the driving force for so long that it will not be put to rest easily. This is where vigilance and discernment are of utmost importance: the way to distinguish truth from illusion, the voice of ego from the voice of the womb, is by the quality of its tone.

The ego's voice is hurried, familiar, and will cause disturbance to the flow of breath. It will talk in an unrefined harshness that will try to persuade, argue, defend, project, belittle, or manipulate. This language is foreign to the reality of our being.

The womb will soothe, invite, inspire, and will, more often than not, be very surprising in what it has to share. A portal to divine wisdom, the womb will acquire a unique point of view that is separate from the mind's. She will share her own unerring insight in such a distinct voice that it will be impossible to ignore.

The womb has to become the master, for it is the creator and the voice of divine wisdom. This authority must be respected and acted upon without delay. When the womb receives consistent nurturance and unconditional love, it starts to come alive, and begins to attune to its vastness and energetic subtleties. If a woman is attentive to the awakening presence of her womb, she will experience new and unique sensations.

Sometimes the womb itself experiences deep, orgasmic pulses, bursts, or waves. These *wombgasms* are different from vaginal or even full-body orgasms. The yoni, too, becomes a highly sensitive instrument, able to receive and transmit even nonphysical information to a partner.

In following the voice of her newly awakened womb, a woman may make some dramatic shifts, suddenly feeling guided to changing her spirituality, her lifestyle, her diet, and even relationships that do not serve her further unfolding. The womb becomes exquisitely sensitive to tastes, feelings, and sensations. These pleasurable feelings can literally be felt in the womb as bursts of palpable loving energy, or living light.

These are feelings that surpass comprehension and are experienced uniquely by each woman. They can be described as orgasmic, magical, ripe, holy, pleasurable, passionate, and blissful. For a woman to feel these mysterious and divine sensations in her womb is a blessing and a gift. It is here that the womb becomes the holiest of shrines, a sacred space where bliss, life, and joy are birthed. One can only surrender to the unknowable play of love that the womb contains: one can never know it.

Man and the Grail Womb

Deep Healing for the Wounded Warrior

MEN ARE THE WOUNDED WARRIORS who yearn to return to the womb for healing. They seek to reconnect to the source of all life by being emotionally present in their hearts. A woman's open womb energy can help a man to grow very quickly. The womb pulls out certain energies from him that can rarely be accessed in other circumstances; this pulling out draws him further into the womb space, where his deepest wounds can be seen and healed.

This healing can be a dramatic and deep process for men, as it involves primal, preverbal energies that connect soul to soul, and that the personality cannot really understand. It dredges up the unresolved subconscious urges within him, bringing to the surface all that has been left unexpressed. All these untended needs, wants, and longings arise, and are resolved, which results in the birthing of a new man, complete in his essential polarities.

This process can be a struggle, as a man may not understand what is happening to him. Even if he does understand it, he may not know how to deal with it, so deep are the subconscious holes and healings. He is likely to experience strong emotions, and will have the work of understanding why they arise and how to work through them. In this way he may discover the powerful combination within himself of consciousness and sexual energy; these will lead him to remember the energy of creation itself—where he comes from, and the place to which he will return.

In many ancient teachings there are five primary emotions: anger, fear, sadness, love, and joy. Each person will identify most strongly with one of these emotions, and also with one the negative emotions: resentment, helplessness, abandonment, loneliness, and grief.

These five primary emotions are formed from the creation point of the womb. Also found here is the energy of male–female union, which operates even when you are not physically making love. In Tibet and in Egypt, the purification and activation of the womb was a precursor to engaging in holy union. This union has been described in many cultures throughout time and is known by many names, including *sacred marriage, yab-yum,* and the *hieros gamos*.

In this union, the physical act of intercourse simultaneously creates a spiritual union. The masculine penetrates the goddess with his love— his vital, sexual energy, his soul, his power, and his ability to activate the birthing and creative aspects of the womb—to bring into being limitless creative potential; to manifest the unmanifest seeds held within his partner's womb. The feminine comes fully into her power by embracing and encircling the man with her heart, and fully opening her yoni and womb to him.

One cannot fully experience sustained union without the womb being open; you can receive glimpses of it, but not sustain it, as an unhealed womb will simply close down if there are still wounds there. In order to be fully empowered, the masculine must feel as though he is being embraced and surrounded by the loving feminine field. A man stands in the center of his strength by using his lingam, heart, and crown as a conduit for light, love, and power, while receiving this gift of being embraced in the heart.

Magnetically alluring, the feminine is able to hold all the power and light that the man has to offer, receiving it completely into her open, healed womb in order to transmute, heal, and—together with her beloved—enter its depths.

Men are deeply affected by women's separation from their essence. If humanity was in accord with nature through the feminine, there would be no ecological crisis, no greenhouse disaster, no raping of the earth's resources for a quick financial fix, and no wars. If women refused to be with the men who propagated such horrors, they would not occur. Women have a power they are not using, and are not even aware of not using. If a woman stopped her husband from going to war, refusing to make love with him if he violated this law of love, do you think he would? Whose authority would he bow to: his wife's, the mother of his children, his partner and co-creator in life, or a politician sitting in the White House?

Women: Stand up! You have the power to change this world, so much power, joy, and love to share. And the ironic thing is that the men are actually waiting for this power, womb power, to be shown to them, for it is a deep part of them also, a part they have forgotten. When they feel it, they too will change. It is because they are not feeling the womb power from the women around them that they feel they can run amok and create a lopsided world built on short-term advantage and selfish gain. Only womb power can stop this, for only this depth, this feeling, can bring a man into true resonance with the feminine within him, reminding him of his essential nature, the nature of the soul.

A COLLECTIVE WOUND

Author Lisa Sarasohn describes the cycle of men's wounding and healing as follows:

> In order to approximate a sense of wholeness, a man projects his own rejected "womanly" ways of being onto the screen of a female that he can (or thinks he can) control. As a result, he no longer perceives that

woman to be a self-determining, self-validating person. In his world, the female human being must be . . . assigned to model his fantasy of what a woman should be. Accordingly, the man's interactions with the woman become a power struggle, a skirmish between "me" and "the parts of me I disown and still yearn to integrate." Isolated in such narcissism, he's unable to recognize the other's autonomy, and is unable to enter into authentic, intimate relationship.

The Asian healing arts refer to a man's hara as his "palace of essence." As a man develops his hara-power, he reaffirms and repossesses the "womanly" qualities he had previously disowned. He begins to perceive a woman as a person, informed by her own purpose. His need to control her diminishes. He becomes more capable of entering into a relationship of mutual respect. As men increasingly live and breathe from center, they prepare themselves to enter into the egalitarian relationships many women desire, and deserve. Truly loving relationships can develop as the partners each live from their inner source of being and support each other in returning to their core wisdom, again and again.*

INNOCENCE

The flow of Shakti creates a sense of innocence for both men and women. A man living in his flow of Shakti constantly discovers what it really means to be a man. And a woman who lives in the flow also discovers anew, in every moment and interaction, what it means to be a woman. Shakti is continuously discovered and released in every moment, unconstricted by the past or the future, or by beliefs about what you think is, was, or could be. This is Original Innocence.

For most individuals the whole idea of being a man or being a woman is so fixed that there is no sense of innocence, or of exploration. The most effective way to sustain innocence is in a relationship, where

---

*Lisa Sarasohn, *The Woman's Belly Book: Finding Your True Center for More Energy, Confidence, and Pleasure* (Novato, Calif.: New World Library, 2006).

there are apparently two "I's" operating. Surrendering your "I" in relating entails a letting go; your sexual energy becomes free of attachment, compulsion, push and pull, instead being moved by holy desire for healing, giving, and loving union. This loving union is best expressed in man and woman when they are whole, and not needing anything from the other. When there is no need, giving and receiving become simultaneous, and the circuit fulfills itself.

SHAKTI IN THE MASCULINE SIDE OF US

A man who has opened himself to feminine energies loves Shakti passionately. To such a man, each partner is the representation of Shakti, and he chooses to serve her, to give and receive simultaneously. His lingam becomes a tool to receive the exquisite vibrations of loving tenderness that he gives to Shakti. He has no ideas about what Shakti is; he just allows it to do as it pleases through him. His mind is situated unwaveringly on her flow, and her flow to him is music that sways in rhythm and tempo. He invites the flow of more Shakti in whomever he meets by seeing the other's music, and adjusting it to Shakti's tempo.

A man who knows Shakti worships her by calling her names out to others. He recognizes the beauty of Shakti in many forms, serving each in whatever way he can, at any moment. He is an empty vessel for Shakti to flow through, listening closely to her voice, obeying her wishes, and following her flow. He lives in the paradox, but not in the mystery, for to him all is revealed. He can move gracefully between his masculine and feminine aspects in the underlying current of giving. He feels emotion deeply, yet is not sucked into it. He shares openly in relationship, expressing vulnerability from a space of tenderness and strength, knowing that his openness can only give rise to more love.

A man in the flow of Shakti is not afraid to use the sword of dissolution, and is not afraid to use the flower of tenderness as, and when, each is required. He can let go and is committed rather than attached to whatever he does, and to whatever relationship he engages in. He serves the will of Shakti, which is to move through the dark and the light with no preference for either, but using each one to liberate us from the ideas and judgments, comparisons and contrasts, we make about reality.

A man who allows himself to resonate with Shakti lives by her rhythm. In his receptivity he finds her voice, and becomes more of a man. In her flow, he wears and sheds different forms—skins to serve the one flowing, the one song. He becomes her servant and lover, and she becomes his mother, sister, and lover. He surrenders to her, and becomes the wielder of Shakti. Together they generate and reveal all of creation.

Divine Masculine Prayer

I Vow to Defend
from the thoughts of the lower self, in both you
    and me
I Vow to Uphold
the feminine values and being
I Vow to Honor
listening to you, and surrendering to your wisdom
    through my actions
I Vow to Protect
the family, the home, and the sanctity of the
    womb we live in.

The Fifth Gate

Union of Sex and Soul

Through the mandala of inner sacred union, the Sacred Marriage of the inner male and female aspects of oneself, lies the rite of passage to enter Me. (T.A.)

THROUGH DEEP PRACTICE WITH THE eighteen pathways of the Shakti Circuit, you begin to embody more and more of the Divine Woman, preparing for the final initiation, which is to become the Divine Woman through sacred union with the Divine Man. This happens when the eighteen pathways have been cleared, healed, and connected. When the pathways have been activated in this way, union can occur inside and out: on the inside through inner practice, and on the outside through sexual union. If you are not currently in a relationship, rest assured; the right man will come as he will be attracted inexorably by the pull of Shakti and the open womb.

The union of man and woman, both inner and outer, is what the fifth gate holds. The combining of any two polarities allows the two to work as one, in this case, rapidly accelerating the fire of consciousness. The body and sexuality are tools through which we experience duality/separation and unity/love. Sexual union, practiced as a rite and an art, is a bridge to the Divine and to other dimensions. In this union, intercourse becomes a sacrament, a living ceremony of bliss, love, and power.

Sacred sexuality is when both partners meet in the infinity loops between their chakras, and in the unique circuit they define together. As this union occurs, dimensional doorways are opened between you and your partner. It is not just about releasing energy through orgasm; it is about staying within the infinity loop as love, attention, and sensual passion flow between you and your partner in one dance. In this union, if there is true harmony and compatibility between you, then your evolution will accelerate exponentially, each of you receiving the deepest lesson/energy you need from the other to complete the wholeness of yourself.

YAB-YUM

The Sacred Marriage practices taught in Egypt and in Tibet were known as *yab-yum*. The yab-yum is the highest of all sacred sexual practices—a set of movements, breaths, and infinity loops that merge sex and soul together. In yab-yum, the two lovers generate an energetic vesica piscis. The female learns to receive and integrate the male, while the male experiences and lets go into the womb of the female. In this exchange, the woman becomes the embodiment of the feminine creative powers. Her womb becomes the physical embodiment of the Grail, with the intent consciously set toward spiritual expansion and nurturance of love, wisdom, power, and the chakras. The man becomes pure consciousness. He penetrates and fertilizes matter with his light and power, while receiving bliss and revitalization through the womb of his Shakti.

Many tantric divinities are represented as being in union with consorts, and these forms are known as *yab-yum* (father-mother) forms. Their union represents the inseparability of relative and absolute, manifestation and void, method and wisdom. They also symbolize

Yab-yum

the union of the 'solar' and 'lunar' energies, the two poles of subtle energy that flow in the subtle energy system of the human body, called the "Inner Mandala." When negative and positive circuits are joined in a lightning circuit, a lamp can be lit.*

Yab-yum circulates sexual energy and light throughout all chakras, subtle bodies, and the subtle energy pathways called *nadis*. This circulation means that all polarities and dualities meet and recognize each other, in order that they may dissolve and flow into loving emptiness. Yab-yum can be done with a partner, or as part of inner Tantra for the solo practitioner.

---

*Chogyal Namkhai Norbu, *The Crystal and the Way of Light: Sutra, Tantra and Dzogchen* (Ithaca, N.Y.: Snow Lion Publications, 1999).

It is through yab-yum with an open and inviting womb that both man and woman can fully heal and transmute many of their deepest blocks. In this deepest of all connections possible between a man and woman, all arises to be seen and potentially transformed—if both partners are able to be emotionally responsible and giving. This is often not the case! However, if both partners have reached a degree of self-responsibility and love within themselves, transmutation can occur through giving.

When you are whole within yourself you no longer need anything to fill you up, to make you whole; you do not need anything from the other. This is the sign the womb is waiting for to fully open the fourth and fifth gates. When a womb feels true unconditional love and solid presence from a man, and these remain steady for a period of time, the womb will open.

When a woman's gates are open from yoni to womb, she takes the man inside to her cosmic womb, where infinite bliss and power lie. Here many temptations can arise, yet only a womb that totally trusts a loving, clear, conscious man will allow him into this space.

Yab-yum done with intimacy and love in this way collects and coagulates the disparate fragments of the shadow. What this means is that unresolved aspects of abuse, trauma, and deep sufferings on a transpersonal level get condensed into archetypal thought-forms (such as animals, demons, or mythical creatures that lie deep within the collective mindset of humanity), which can then be transmuted through Tantric healing. This condensation vastly accelerates the healing process—what needed therapy for one year can be done in one hour, and what defies rational or even transpersonal explanations and processes can be dissolved rapidly.

Yab-yum allows the man to regenerate and strengthen himself, uniting his lightbodies into form through the vehicle of the *ka* lightbody, or interface between the dimensions. This is what Yeshua did with Magdalene to prepare himself for his crucifixion. Yab-yum allows the woman to do this also, to be her cosmic self and embody the Divine Woman more fully.

Yab-yum in its full form unites sexual energy with the light-body, until there is no separation between the two. In this deepest of Tantras, breath and movement cease, and all that is left is spaciousness and loving bliss. This is a process of soul merging, a deep sharing of soul blueprints and information between you and your partner that leads to deeper and deeper levels of intimacy. Flesh merges with flesh, and spirit with spirit. All boundaries dissolve.

Intimacy allows us to be so in tune with a partner that we may feel his or her pleasures, sadness, thoughts, and intentions even if we are many thousands of miles away. It is in the lightbody—when it merges with your physical body and sexual energy as one flow—that you can completely give yourself to your partner, or to Spirit. When two lightbodies connect, we merge with the other into pure space. This bonding at all levels transcends physical, sexual, and spiritual ideas and programming about what relationships are, or should be.

In this process of connecting on the most profound levels, old wounds, abuses, mistrusts, and barriers to such complete relationship may arise. You may feel that you are losing yourself in your partner or forming a deep aversion or attachment. You may feel like running away; you may feel mother or father issues arising strongly or old wounds resurfacing to be looked at again.

It is at this point that a true relationship or sacred marriage can occur. What is required is for these wounds to be met with embrace and honesty, communication, and appreciation. You must feel that you are being fully received, by yourself and by your partner. In true intimacy there are no more barriers, no more shields—you are both totally naked and exposed in all ways.

It is in the balance and harmony achieved through the sacred marriage of your masculine and feminine that carries you through the fifth gate, and opens you fully to the field of living light between the fifth and sixth gates, wherein lie the seed jewels of the womb.

THE JEWELS OF
YOUR SOUL'S PURPOSE

One of the most important events of your lifetime is to remember what you came here to do, and why you decided to incarnate into your present body, environment, parents, and country. With this knowledge you can guide your life in the direction you long for, fulfill the deepest desires of your heart and soul, and achieve the highest potential you have as a human being.

The majority of humanity is not fulfilling its karmic contracts—not doing the tasks they wanted to do before incarnation, and that they agreed to do to help the world. This widespread failure to keep karmic commitments is the cause of much confusion and frustration that can be felt almost everywhere in the world today. Spiritual seeking without knowledge of your soul's purpose is ungrounded; such work can lead you in circles, like a hamster running a constant loop in a small cage. Here, the hamster is your soul trying to remember who it is, while it is trapped in the cage of the ego, running around on the wheel of reincarnation. Until you remember and put into action your soul's purpose, you will be the hamster forever running around in a self-enclosed circle, seeking and never finding.

Finding your soul's purpose is perhaps one of the most important tasks facing you today. Once you find it and consciously activate it with loving willpower and wisdom, the whole world will conspire to help you to achieve it, to lead you into the greatest love you can know.

Your first forgetting of your soul's purpose occurred upon birth, where you developed divine amnesia that caused you to lose memory of who you are, and what you came here to do. Some memory was likely revealed to you when you were a child, but your developing ego quickly dismissed these remembrances, due to parental and peer group pressures which labeled your innocent remembering as fantastical, impractical, or improbable.

The first steps to remembering can include practices to become self-aware: meditation, breath work, witnessing thoughts and emotions, and so forth. The quieter the mind becomes, the more we are able to listen to the still, small voice of the heart and soul that always knows why we are here, and what we are here to do.

The next steps can include remembering how you came into the world before birth, your experiences in the womb, and then of being physically born into this world. As this healing and wisdom arise to be integrated, you can engender your own rebirthing via the journey into the seven gates, and the connection to the Galactic Center found within us.

The seed jewels of your soul's purpose lie in a field of living light that exists in the womb between the fifth and sixth gates. Each woman holds her own unique soul jewels here—her soul's mission, and the means to achieve it on Earth. These soul-purpose jewels are usually several in number and can take many forms. They are often well guarded by trauma or deep blocks for which there seem to be no explanation or healing available. Yet there is an innate knowing, deep within you, that there is something else here . . . something you cannot quite put your finger on, but something you have been waiting for.

As you travel into the eighteen pathways, healing, opening, and activating them, these seed jewels come to light. They can manifest in the womb in many ways: they may look like jewels, keys, orbs of light, scrolls of wisdom, songs, even a baby. And each manifestation is perfect for each person. The jewels lie within: count them as you see them. Travel into them, see what they are, ask them what they are and how they can be made manifest. Each jewel is a seed potential, a part of your soul desiring to bloom, activate, and rise into manifestation. Every human holds these jewels inside.

The Sixth Gate

Surrender to the Power of Shakti

In the space between the fifth and sixth gates, a woman, like the Dakinis and priestesses of ancient tradition, can open herself in service to any man and bring a great healing and transformation for him. This means surrendering yourself completely to a physical man—allowing him to penetrate your very soul on all levels.

By holding the intent within yourself to give freely, allowing through your love and surrender to transform and transmute his pain, his suffering, his ancient wounds—you both receive. He will receive the powerful gift of transmutation from the Divine Mother through you as a vessel, and this in turn can enable you to pass beyond the sixth gate. To pass beyond the gate together, he, too, must be in the same surrendered, giving space of service, and capable of reaching sacred union within himself. (T.A.)

TO ACTIVATE AND MANIFEST THE sixth gate fully requires surrender. Surrendering to the power of Shakti as it is comes through you means you are open to life, regeneration, and the laws and beauty of nature. Surrendering to love's will is where you discover that love is God, and God is love. Surrender is the final feminine wisdom key to awakening.

Surrendering to what is presented to you in life brings up your deepest resistance, your deepest shadows. Everything in the basement of your subconscious, every voice within you that says no to love, no to peace, no to joy, no to what is, arises, and fights. This fight takes you deeper and deeper, and wears you out, wears out the fight in you, the resistances of the small self, until you break down. In this breaking down lies the opening to the softness and gentling of love. Surrender dismantles every part of you, and remakes you in love's image, but only when you have sincerely asked for love to enter your life.

Surrender softens what is rigid within. It gentles us, taking us deeper into the silence of the still, open heart that is awake and sensitive to all that is not love. Awakening guides us back from the edge of not-love, by embracing and forgiving all thoughts and feelings that arise.

Even when you think you are surrendered there is more; there is always more. Surrender is a process, a continual experience that happens every day. It is never done or completed, never a statement. One is always surrendering, continually giving over the mind to what lies here and now, in each thought, each choice.

Surrender leads to true vulnerability, which cleanses the heart and releases fear. Letting go of fear we are able to expand into more love, which in turn leads to more vulnerability and more fears arising . . . until all that is left is a pure heart as a conduit for love to flow through—life as a moment-by-moment surrender. You move when the palpable living force of love moves you, because you have become so available, so present in the open heart, that you live by what you know to be true, because it is happening right now.

Surrender also requires meditation in order for it to be whole. It is wise guided action, spontaneous and in the now, without fear, belief, expectation, or hope. There is no surrender to something; you surrender unto Being. This is the true nature of the action of Shakti. In this trust, nothing matters because everything changes completely every moment. All your sense of reason and planning collapses. Everything that is needed right now might be completely different from what was needed in the previous moment, and in the next moment. Love responds in the now, and there is no teaching, laws, or rules for this. Love is the whole of the law.

THE OPEN CONDUIT

Only when there is nothing else that you want from the dream of the world will you be free, and this is surrender. If you are totally surrendered, awake and alive, your heart is the conduit through which you and others receive abundance. In surrender all things are given through you.

You have to completely release the little self and the dream of "getting" in order to be open, and in this release you become quite attractive—a magnet that draws to you ten times what you have given. You do what you need to do, with care, with full attention, and then move on to the next thing to do, which unfolds organically.

This step-by-step approach allows the full death of the previous moment in order to create space for the next new moment, where we know nothing about the future, and have forgotten about the past. This involves deep trust that whatever is needed will come, that the unfolding will take you wherever you need to go. And this is the mystery that dissolves the "I." Any thoughts of "I, me, mine," or "I deserve this or need that," any validation of there being a separate self that needs any justification, gets continually surrendered and given to God.

The mind plays its role as the servant of the soul, allowing the observation and surrender of any and all ideas of "I." This letting go is a literal emptying of the self in order to give yourself space to Be. Letting go again and again of the "I" in the midst of your thoughts, deeds, and interactions with others shows you how you are still holding onto the idea of being a separate person needing something for itself. This letting go is an inner action, a movement on your part that recognizes the ideas and wants of a personal self, and lets go of it in the same moment. To die to this self means to die to all self-talk, self-importance, self-validation, and the projection of yourself out into the world.

Through our surrender to being here, to embracing all aspects of life, we become one with the creation. Everything is included in surrender, and nothing is left out. All that you have believed and experienced has to be offered, and given away. Everything has to go, and you have to leave no back door, no escape route, no way for the small self to come back.

Everything you know to be true has to be placed in the heart, and given to love, to do what love wills. This surrender creates a vast opening, a space where you can be pulled—where love can pull you—and take you to your destination, wherever that may be.

Surrender is the last quality to master you before you live the surrendered life. Living a surrendered life, there are few thoughts arising within you. You may not know the words that will come out of your mouth in any moment, and have no need to remember what they are, or what the actions are that flow through your bodymind and speech. You learn by what comes through you. There is great delight and joy in this, for in this allowing of ourselves to be nobody, we become able to relate with anybody, in any moment.

SURRENDER AS SERVICE

Surrender is the portal through which love and Shakti flow; it is the conduit that allows love to pour through us more and more as we abandon the notion of a separate self, bound in dual voices. The acceptance and allowance of everything that is happening to you right now leads, by extension, to an acceptance of everything that is happening in the world around you, locally and globally. This surrender does not lead to passivity, but to an ever-present thread of contentment, a state of fluid peace that is the basis for awakened and radical action in the world.

The more surrendered we are, the more responsible we become, as we start to understand that the world's troubles are also part of our own, and that we have to do something about them. We become busier and more passionate as Shakti flows more and more, for now what flows spontaneously through us are actions that serve others as extensions of our own self. As we are surrendered, there is nothing else left to do apart from this. Surrender is how Shakti manifests in us all; it is the open gate for God to walk into us.

Whereas surrender is the source of harmony, contention is the root of discord. When one is in contention, one is not in surrender. Surrender is recognizing the difference between the presence of flow and the absence of flow. Life lives through us, love masters us, and the adventure of life carries us along, moment by magical moment.

NAMAH:
THE SOUND OF SURRENDER

Namah is the sound of surrender and the sound of connection. It has seven different layers of meaning, resonance, and embodiment. As the ending of most Sanskrit mantras, *namah* sends energy to the aspect of the Divine that one is connecting with by fully opening yourself to, and surrendering to it. *Namah* within a mantra is the sound of surrender to the Shakti, the energy of the quality of the Divine, and the life flow that animates and enlivens the mantra.

Namah is correctly pronounced with the *"ah"* at the end of the word having a sibilant out-breath that sends life force out into silence, into the gap between thoughts where manifestation of the Divine occurs.

The first layer of meaning of *namah* is the most commonly known: to bow down to God. The second meaning is to pay obeisance to, or pay your dues to God, in the hope of dissolving karmas and attaining more humility. The third is to offer something, or to desire something from God in hope of attaining something of material or egoic benefit.

The fourth level is to open up to God, humbly and in reverence, from the soul. The fifth level is to surrender your soul to God's will, to allow the Shakti to flow as it wishes beyond your control and conscious awareness and desire. The sixth level of meaning of *namah* is to open up and surrender your soul without limits; *na* = without, *mah* = limits.

Without wanting for self, or needing to gain anything for self, simply offering oneself as a conduit through which the Divine can act for the highest benefit.

The ego is working on the first three levels of *namah*. The soul takes over on the next two levels. God itself is the sixth and seventh levels of *namah,* where the soul surrenders its identity or higher self into God.

Within *namah* is the basis of the spiritual path. As one journeys through life, working, and healing, the ego starts to become the servant of the soul. At this point, selfless service, love, and joy become the foundations of your life. As you move forward, the soul becomes more dissolved in deeper states of peace that require a deeper effort to attain, for the soul is now happy to reside in itself. The soul can get stuck at this time, and it takes a great effort to move beyond this point of soul contentment, which is still not enlightenment.

As the soul moves deeper into peace, the mind that is part of the soul gets dismantled so that so the breath of Shakti can dissolve it completely. In truth, the ego is a servant of God, designed to accomplish organizational, linear, and mundane tasks as an automatic response.

The seventh resonance of *namah* is to become Shakti, the breath of the Divine, to embody Shakti and transmit its divine qualities. This seventh level is the difference between a priest/ess and a high priest/ess. The priest/ess makes offerings and petitions in the service of God for people who wish to attain something. The high priest/ess embodies God and transmits its transformative or healing power directly to those who are sincere and ready to receive.

ALONENESS

Aloneness describes the way that we are each alone on the path; what fulfills us most comes from within. As we take full responsibility for our fulfillment, we become whole—no longer demanding that the context of our lives provide us happiness, or hoping to view our wholeness through anyone else's eyes. You come to see that no relationship can cause you to be unloving or harsh, for you are alone, all one, in your journey to God.

This aloneness creates spaciousness, depth, and genuineness, because you no longer feel a need to look or act in any way shaped by the world. You no longer value what the world thinks, but create your own value. Paradoxically, such aloneness allows you to become closer to every person, and allows every person to feel closer to you. You have dismantled any barriers to closeness and people can feel that; it speaks to their hearts and attracts them.

FLUID JOY

Reality is fluid and open. When love is required it flows; when joy is required that too flows; when ruthless compassion is needed it too flows. What may serve you in one moment may not serve you in the next. This fluidity dissolves all rules, allowing you to express and embody the highest potential in any moment. This is resting in the heart of harmony. This resting, this abiding, is natural and graceful, and cannot be forced. It arises the more we tune into the harmony of our heart's voice over time, and follow it in action.

Home is where the heart is, and we enter our home through surrender. This home is shadowless joy, soul-felt, all-inclusive, and shared with others; it is the joy that flows when you feel the happiness of others, and the joy that flows for no reason. This is the pulse constantly humming in all life, that we feel spontaneously undulating throughout all parts of us, and in the life around us.

When surrender has mastered your life, you live at your own innermost urging, the calling of your heart's desire. You follow your inner voice, and listen to your natural rhythms as they harmonize with the earth, your loved ones, and life itself. Living in a way that keeps you connected to this core leads to perpetual joy. Such joy is always here when you need it; all you have to do to access it is let go of anything standing in the way.

Creation manifests in a flash, in a pulse of pure joy, spontaneous and free of any distinct purpose, like a thief in the night. To reach this stage of joy is a major turning point, for it is only here that true life begins. For the first time we are ready to fully incarnate, to fully "land on the planet," and be happy without a trace of fear, judgment, or any significant residue from prior states. At this level life is fully guided by synchronicity, intuition, and grace. Sudden bursts of joy for no reason overcome you. In true joy, we feel no separation between ourselves and life itself, for joy opens the door, and welcomes all of life NOW.

The Seventh Gate

The Infinite Well and the Grail

THE SEVENTH GATE IS THE Grail within, where everything stops and revels in the deep silence before creation. What all men have been searching for lies here: the return to source. What all women are beginning to remember, their power and their unique feminine spiritual pathway, lies here also. What unites man and woman is the Grail; the pathway to eternal life, the life borne from spirit, the life lived in the present, not the past; the life lived as miraculous and magical every day, as natural, and normal.

Within the seventh gate lies the power of transformation on a core level. The Grail is the Black Light, the light that washes you clean of your small self, that washes you into the eternal, that brings you the experience of the infinite from deep within your bodymind. (For more about the Black Light, see page 213.

It is in the seventh gate that female Samadhi happens: the breath within the womb stops, the mind stops, the fear of death stops, and you are left totally present, totally natural. You become unadorned simplicity, able to sit in the moment where all creation starts, and stops.

It is here that you go within for your fuel, the limitless flow in the swelling river of being. It is here that eternity lies, from which all is birthed, from which Shakti flows—the doorway to the great Central

Sun, to God. As above, so below: the great Central Sun at the center of our galaxy, the Great Womb prophesied by the Mayans as meeting us in 2012, lies within you right now. Not in the future, but here and now. Why wait for it when it is here now?

As you traveled through the sixth gate, you learned how to use all the aspects of the eighteen pathways, and how to transmute the blockages that stop you from venturing deeper into your feminine essence. It demanded tremendous courage to pass through here, for we can only go as far as our longing can reach: our longing, our passion, and our desire for the Ultimate.

The silence of the seventh gate is accessed as we find light in the heart of darkness to lead us to our core. To get there, we are required to travel far from ordinary experience. Here there is nothing familiar, no matrix world, and no realm of dreams—just silence. Here lies what is ignored or glossed over by most humans.

THE VOICE OF
THE SEVENTH GATE

I am nurturer, the One who Nourishes all.
I am Fertile, the sacred ground in which the Creator entrusts the Seeds
  of life to unite, germinate and grow.
I am Cycle, and the Circle of Life.
I have no beginning. I have no end.
I am Vast Space, the infinite spaciousness of Divine Consciousness.
I am Sacred Waters, the ever-flowing Waters of the Ocean of Creation.
I am Chosen, the Gifted One, designated to Receive and to Cradle the
  Inspirations of the Heavenly Cosmic Mind.

I am home. Your first house.
It is my wish that You remember.
You can return to me always,
for rest and comfort, peace, protection.

I am Invitation, the invitation to the great Earthly Dance of ecstatic love.
I am Power beyond Measure. Of Source, not Force. (T.A.)

Your Experiences

For all this power I have been feared, scorned, subjugated, abused,
repressed, silenced, maimed by all of those incapable of feeling the fullness
of my reflection within themselves. Under such potent assault I would find
myself with other womb-men disconnecting from the burning fires of my
passion, and in an attempt to preserve the precious embers even became
icy; either frigid within my own sexual force, or frozen away from the
natural swaying or seductive or ecstatic movement of my inner dance.

My deep sadness is that I in turn have responded to this by withdrawing,
shutting myself off to the outside, and often times even to myself. This
contraction has been most painful. My inner agony indeed, and disruptive
to the natural flow of things.

The fabric of humanity is waking up now to the great remembrance of
the medicine of the warm waters of my dark void, where pulsing primal
rhythms can always be felt and heard, calling us up, and comforting us
back. Encouraging us to take our very first breath on our own in every
moment . . . again . . . and again . . . and again.

Everyone always honors the Divine Mother externally as if it was outside
themselves, when in fact, it always has been, and always will be, right here.
You are Isis, just as Magdalene, just as Mother Mary were. This is the
truth of the Isis teachings, now resurrecting once again. (K.M.)

In the eternal space of the womb, my breath was lost within the peace as
we moved through the seventh gate. My body no longer needed to breathe
in from outside. All was within, for I became the breath. Within this Black
Light are the seeds of life, pure potentiality, awaiting my surrender to Divine
Will, the re-membering of my dharma, my role to enact in this divine play.
Reminded of time/space and bringing the breath into my left ovary, I
returned to breathing with my body as my consciousness became the nozzle

for the pump to fuel the burning fires of my ovaries from the Source, beyond the threshold of the seventh gate, the Filling Station. (C.O.)

With the increase in the flow, the gates fly open as you approach, ready to expand even further. The filling station at the seventh gate is already streaming light into your being as you pass the gates. Your continued presence with this practice will enable you to carry even greater light into the womb of the world, intensifying your capacity as a beacon. In the circular flow of giving and receiving, as you in service bring this greater light, so will more be able to be shared with you, which in turn enhances your ability to give and be in service to an even greater degree.

Do you see the divine beauty of the unfolding as you connect through me?

This is the divine secret that has been lost to humanity and has resulted in their intense separation. If all could accept, hear, and practice this knowledge, all would feel themselves pulled along towards God on this ever upward spinning spiral of giving and receiving. This beautiful journey is the key to your homecoming, and yet you are the one's who chose to not only ignore it, but to forget it was ever possible. (T.A.)

Once you have explored the deeper meanings of the seven gates, you can return to them any time to continue the work of opening and healing them. The following meditation practice is a good way to prepare for the deeper journey.

♣ Seven Gates Meditation
Preparing to Open the Gates

1. Sit quietly and bring your attention to your heart.
2. Hold the tip of the little finger of the right hand with your left thumb, index, and middle fingers. You should have two fingers over your right little fingernail.
3. Sit and breathe into your heart through pursed lips. When you

feel energy coming into your heart, allow it to become more intense. Really feel the heart. It may begin to feel tingly, hot, or full; just be with it for a few breaths longer.

4. Begin now to breathe and direct the energy to go into your womb. Feel your womb being cleared, healed, and opened.

5. Now breathe all the energy up to the top of the spine, the Alta Major.

6. See a golden ball here, and feel it releasing what is no longer needed, and receiving divine energy.

7. When you have a sense of this ball being fully activated, bring it up to the pineal gland situated between the center of the eyes in the middle of the brain. Breathe the energy now to activate the brain and "light up" this gland.

8. Now place one hand over the heart, and one over the womb. These are your two hearts. Feel a figure-8 of gold light connecting your two hearts. Breathe gently.

Note: This last section can be done at any time to reassure and comfort yourself.

The First Gate

Start by focusing on the entrance to the first gate, the lips of the yoni, the lips of love. This is where you allow energies in, and where you give energies out. The yoni is the opening into the infinite. You may physically touch any of the gates as you deepen, and breathe into it.

Visualize a pure white conch with the Goddess arising from it.

What do you feel here?

What colors, sensations, feelings are here?

What is her real form and shape?

What does she want to say to you?

What specifically does she want from you to open and connect to the other gates?

How does she want you to recognize and honor her?

The Second Gate

Start by focusing on the second gate: the Gratitude-spot, the waters of ecstasy and freedom.

Visualize a streaming blue waterfall, wild and free.

What is its sound?

What do you feel here?

What colors, sensations, feelings are here?

What is her real form and shape?

What does she want to say to you?

What specifically does she want from you to open and connect to the other gates?

How does she want you to recognize and honor her?

The Third Gate

Start by focusing on the Third Gate: the clitoris, the rose of pleasure.

Visualize a blooming, red, ripe rose.

What do you feel here?

What colors, sensations, feelings are here?

What is her real form and shape?

What does she want to say to you?

What specifically does she want from you to open and connect to the other gates?

How does she want you to recognize and honor her?

The Fourth Gate

Start by focusing on the fourth gate—the cervix, entrance to the holy of holies, the cosmic womb.

Visualize a diamond opening, the stargate of your cervix. This is the opening into your womb, and an opening into infinite space.

What do you feel here?

What colors, sensations, feelings are here?

What does she want to say to you?

What specifically does she want from you to open, and connect to her, and the womb?

How does she want you to recognize and honor her?

The Fifth Gate

Enter pure vast space. Visualize the yab-yum or Sacred Marriage, the holy lovemaking union between the inner male and female aspects of yourself.

Breathe gently into this space. As you go deeper, you start to see many jewels sparkling. Choose one and zoom into it. Ask it what it is. Ask how to manifest it. Each jewel is a seed potential, a seed of your soul purpose.

The Sixth Gate

Visualize a cross within a vesica piscis. Relax, and be silent to whatever arises within you.

The Seventh Gate

Surrender into the eternal womb.

PART TWO

Power in the Womb

The Power of the Womb

Love and Power in the Compassionate Womb

THE POWER OF THE WOMB has been forgotten for millennia. Now that it is resurfacing again as part of the perennial or timeless wisdom, its ability to turn boys into men and girls into women is becoming apparent. This maturing then allows men and women to become kings and queens, or people living in the authority of Sovereign Love. This sovereignty occurs through the union of love and power, the ability of the womb to transmute and heal, the transformation of our biology, and the earth-centered power and majesty of the ancient allies of Shakti: the dragons.

THE DRAGON AND THE WOMB

Dragons have played a part in the history of the world since the beginning. We see them sprinkled throughout ancient traditions where they are often described as purely mythic creatures, but many cultures tell stories of dragons that were real living beings. Some of those traditions have held dragons in high esteem: Hindu and Buddhist teachings, for example, regard the *nagas* as guardians or keepers of secret knowledge.

This knowledge was shared only with devotees or initiates, such as Nagarjuna, one of the most important Buddhist philosophers in history. It was during a meditation at a lake in India that Nagarjuna received secret knowledge from a naga who had been guarding it for him, which he has since shared with millions of Buddhists throughout the ages.

The Tibetan Buddhist monks, as another example, had a regular practice of overtoning near waterfalls specifically to receive help from the water and air dragons in refining their sound and breath. Seen as activators of the life force, the Tantra nagas of Hinduism were an essential component of a student's quest for enlightenment. Even the Buddha was often pictured with serpents and dragons surrounding him. It is said that the empress or queen of the nagas recognized the Buddha and appeared before him, saluting him as an avatar prior to his enlightenment.*

In Arthurian times, Merlin and Arthur Pendragon worked with these guardians to bring justice, peace, prosperity, and reconciliation between humans, the earth, and the elemental and heavenly forces. Later however, the Christian tradition grew to fear these beings and the unbridled, feminine energies they represented. Unable to control these energies, Christian leaders chose instead to wipe their memory out completely. Pagan nature worshipers, druids, priestesses, witches, and anything associated with the Divine Feminine, Earth, and the dragons, was burned or buried in ongoing acts of repression.

Recent history, in relative terms, has taken us away from this connection and knowledge, building a fear of "reptilian" energy and form, creating the disappearance of the physical dragons that still inhabited the planet and honoring the rising culture of "dragon slayers," by spreading legends of the dragons as hideous, bloodthirsty creatures. Widespread fears expanded to different cultures, and the physical dragons themselves began to disappear, along with all forms of nature worship, Goddess worship, and devic and nature spirit connection. Dragons

---

*Araya with Padma Prakasha, *The Dragon Within,* a 2008 e-book available at www .dragonwithin.com.

were left to exist only in legends and stories, until the time was right for their resurgence, when humanity would be ready to remember and work with them again. That time is now.

It is important to turn now and look again at the many forms that Earth wisdom takes, and open our hearts in order to recognize where we truly come from, so that we may pass into the next level of understanding. Our flow of life, abundance, creativity, and freedom are connected to working with these dragon energies in a conscious way. Shakti is also dragon power. It is through our connection to the dragon energies, which are becoming available once again, that our lightbodies can be fully grounded into the physical dimension. This is why the dragons are resurfacing, and why they play such a crucial role at this time on the planet. This resurgence comes at a time when the return of the Divine Feminine is also ripe, because these two developments are inextricably linked to each other: it is through the dragon lines that the energies among our human body (DNA), our lightbody (soul), and Gaia (nature) can be connected and harmonized.

Dragon energy brings up ancient work for us to tap into. Opening deep energetic pathways in the body, dragons can assist us in clearing and healing ancient, stuck debris that cannot be accessed in other ways. Dragons also carry the keys for us to activate the crystalline matrices of our physical bodies, thus allowing us to anchor the lightbody into the physical plane on a permanent basis. Working with the dragon energy opens, activates, and heals the seven gates, allowing you to connect yourself to your body, to your life force, and to the living earth itself.

The Dragon Within

The womb contains a very strong ball of energy, composed of concentrated wisdom, power, and magic as old as the earth itself. At the base of every womb this energy lies sleeping, curled up in the form of a crystalline ball encasing a tiny dragon. When you first see it, the dragon in the womb may appear black or green; the green connects us most deeply with Gaia, the Earth Mother, and the black to Ishtar—the creative, fertile power of the void.*

To activate the womb requires the power of dragon energy, which helps us to clear negative electrical charges, memories, traumas, and shocks of the past through connecting us to the pulse of life. One way to do this is to synchronize ourselves with the leylines or energy pathways of the earth. These leylines are physical manifestations of dragon energy that also connect the earth to cosmic leylines of sound and light emerging from the Galactic Center.

This dragon energy, the primordial force, the serpent power, is a key part of grounding and opening the womb completely. Only the heart can really guide this vibrant, fertile, awakening power. And only the connection between the womb and the heart can make this dragon, this ancient primordial power, really live again.

For most people it is not possible to pass alone through this strong, deep, black energy. We cannot give birth in a state of seclusion, for to give birth means we stay completely in connection with All That Is, with the pain and the death, with the purest joy and love, with it all. When we welcome it, love it, and make love with all parts of being, then a great magic can come true. You can give birth to the mystery of life.

ACTIVATING THE PULSE OF POWER

This Pulse runs throughout all life. It is the primordial throb that gives the power of life to all beings. All Life starts with the pulse of the heart, and ends as the pulse of the heartbeat fades away. The pulse of the heart, pumping life throughout our bodies, minds, and organs is a Pulse of Power when it is allied with the pulse of the womb. When both pulse together in unison a vibrant flow of joy, bliss, and peace moves through the bodymind and soul.

---

*Araya with Padma Prakasha, *The Dragon Within*.

Each heart has a natural tendency to fall into synchrony with the pulse of other hearts. For example, samples of tissue taken from two live hearts will beat in their own rhythms, but when they are laid together, touching, they will begin to beat together. This entrainment to the common pulse is the heartbeat of existence. If we remain in contact with this pulse it is impossible to injure another, for we are both in tune with the same rhythm. We are one, and feel the same things.*

The Pulse of life can become stagnant or stuck within different parts of ourselves. The life force does not move freely from one organ to the next; maybe the womb itself is blocked; perhaps the heart is weak; perhaps the pancreas is wounded. When this happens, we can feel tired, irritated, out of balance, unable to express ourselves fully.

The Pulse aligns us with the body, and opens the body to receive higher energies. As we move the Pulse throughout the bodymind, the heart and belly also open, dissolving layers of inertia into free-flowing joy and vitality. It is a direct way to align yourself with the underlying pulse and synchrony of all life, as all life comes from the Pulse. In the heart and womb lies the Creative Pulse of all life. Life originated from this pulse through an Act of Love, Passion, and Pure Creativity—a Creativity that has no reason to be creative, and no goal for its creation—it just is Creativity by its very nature.

By tuning into this pulse, whether through bodywork, breath, Tibetan pulsing practices, lovemaking, or communing with the earth at sacred sites, we align ourselves back to the primordial power. By doing this our whole system *becomes* the Pulse: our body starts to vibrate, and the cells hum at orgasmic intensity, shaking and releasing our whole being back into the primordial flow. Everything that is not aligned to this free-flowing wave dissolves. Fears transform into bliss, joy, and pleasure.

Individually we each work with the pulse of our own womb and heart. As a species we resonate with one another, and with the pulse at

*Information from private conversation with Susan Richardson of Tibetan Pulsing.

the core of the earth, evidenced in the rotations the earth makes every day and night. On a Galactic scale we attune to the pulse of our Sun and the Central Sun of the galaxy—the Hunab Ku or Timekeeper of the Pulse, as recognized in the Thirteen Moon natural calendar. By synchronizing all these pulses within our bodies, we can tune in to the cosmic pulse.

THE WOMB AS TRANSMUTER

When the womb is clear and open it has the capacity to take in any energy and transform it. Through the womb's nonjudgmental embrace, any emotion, quality, or wound can be transformed. Anger can become vulnerability; hate can become peace; judgment can become forgiveness. The angry man becomes the innocent child, and the viciousness of hate becomes softened into vulnerability and tender embrace. The womb-heart of any woman can become the womb of the Divine Mother, becoming the all-accepting, all-embracing transmuter of fear and negativity. Whatever is thrown at this womb can be embraced and transform into its opposite. This is the next big step for humanity—and for women—to take.

This consciousness within the feminine can see the pain and wounding that lie at the heart of the human experience of separation, while simultaneously seeing each person's essence as divine. This simultaneity leads to the rise of a form of sadness that births compassion as our human imperfection and our divine perfection meet.

The womb-heart makes us feel vulnerable when we return to her in this manner. It opens us up, revealing our deepest fears, wounds, and rage at the separations we feel. It is in returning to the womb that we heal; the wounded warrior returns to be reborn as peace, as compassion. This transmutation can be spontaneous, and a similar process occurs in a male form through the active, fiery Dance of Shiva, the Dance of Transmutation, the dancing upon the corpse of ignorance and forgetting.

The open, activated, fertile womb-heart is a space of magical transformation, where anything becomes possible. Transformation is successful when the issue or problem you thought you have completely dissolves, and you cannot even remember what the issue was. Transformation is not change, or improvement. It is a radical new space and possibility that has never existed before in your life, and which comes into existence by actively emptying the past out of yourself so that you can be present.

In this emptying, whatever you declare with commitment and passion comes into being, for transformation occurs when you enter into an empty space, and then create from this empty space whatever possibility touches, and moves you deeply. If this possibility does not occur, you get broken down in order for you to break through, opening you up to even greater possibilities and transformation.

In the past, suffering could be brought within the womb and transmuted through the embrace of a group of women. The last group of women to do this was the Three Marys: Mother Mary, Magdalene, and Salome. This is also how collective transmutation can be activated—even for a whole planet—if enough women can heal and awaken their wombs. A group of such women aligning with a portal to the womb of the world—like the one in Giza, Egypt—can heal a whole planet by dissolving suffering back into the Source.

Giza is such a powerful portal to the Womb of the World because of the pyramids there, particularly the Isis pyramid. It is this building that the Sphinx protects; he is the Guardian of the Womb of the World. This pyramid has not been active for thousands of years, as most have forgotten its purpose and how to activate it.

Three initiations are possible in the Great Pyramid: one through the Well, the place where you confront your deepest fears; a second in the Queen's Chamber where you harmonize and heal your fears; and the third in the King's Chamber. Here initiates receive entry into the Divine Masculine Christ Consciousness through alignment to fourteen different star systems. Together, these initiations prepare the seeker to work in the next pyramid with the Womb of the World and the Cosmic Mother. Only by completing these three initiations could a seeker be ready to enter the Womb of the World, and to wield the power of creation, manifestation, and dissolution that is held there.

A Womb Speaks

I hold all within me as a piece of the Divine Mother. . . . I do not have to take anything into myself in order to transmute it, for it is already within me simply waiting to be brought forth and thrown into the fires of dissolution. This act simply takes surrender coming from the person or energetic field that is desiring transmutation. Once initiated from their field, my "work" is fairly simple.

The fires of dissolution burn within me at all times ready to receive at the slightest hint of preparedness to surrender. I am in tune with all things and stand ready, catching the thought form almost before it is born because of my eagerness, the eagerness of the Divine Mother, to see her children healed and whole again. The separation has gone too deep and lasted too long and there is a heavy layer of sadness in her heart, our heart, to see the suffering of humanity.

So, ever-ready in service, I sit and watch for sparks to call me into action—my joyous gifts anxious to be taken advantage of for they are powerful and can bring so much healing. Like the touch of Christ, or the healing that flowed from the hems of his robes to those he passed by, and as they reached out believing, asking from their hearts for healing and having the faith that it would be so, so it was.

Imagine something even more powerful than this—that with even a thought-form on the other side of the planet, I can spring into action, because I am in all places at once. I am part of the grid work of Mother Earth and the Divine Mother that are interlaced through every womb.

This is what all wombs have forgotten; their potential as transmuters and their connection to all that Is. They exist in a dark space, but it is not the void of creation, the emptiness of potential. It is a black hole of their own creation, more like a cave with only one entrance to hide in, and only one way out back to their true nature. Hiding in this cave, afraid even to imagine there is light or hope somewhere, their soul sits, alone and separate. If only they will call out, the Divine Mother can instantaneously be there to show them how close the warmth and depth of their own womb space is, and where their True nature lies. (T.A.)

THE COMPASSIONATE WOMB

I am the vessel for creation, the wellspring of life. Within my dark expanse are wells overflowing with wisdom, love, and power. The river of compassion is filled in equal parts from these wells. Enter the darkness of my being for your light to flow more clearly. Allow the purging, experience the density of pain and suffering within and around, yet let it not contain you, nor you be contained by it. (C.O.)

In Aramaic and Hebrew the word *rahme* (also *rahmane* or *rahum*), means love, mercy, and compassion. In the multidimensional tapestry of meaning that all sacred languages contain, *rahum* also means womb, the source of all birth. As we delve even deeper into its meaning we discover *rahum* describes a journey of transformation borne from power and love combined. This is not a passive love, but rather a palpable rebirthing of the self in creative power from the center, the Source.

Uniting within through love and power is to be in direct connection with the breath of God that is Shakti. It is to be willing to feel the soul's immensity, and deep compassion for all suffering. Descending into this space before birth—the deepest space full of Black Light—and arising from it in creative expression, leads us to embody this luminosity more fully.

Compassionate Womb Breathing

In the powerful practice of the Compassionate Womb Breathing, sacred sound codes in Aramaic, the language spoken by Christ, Magdalene, and Mother Mary, merge with deep, rhythmic breathing patterns to activate your womb. This practice realigns you into the infinity loop of creative, loving, and vast energy that connects and heals womb/hara and heart. In the process, you move your center of gravity from the mind to your womb/hara, your true center.*

This cleanses and purges the womb and belly, empowering you directly and unmistakably with the felt sense of your own loving womb power, bringing new direction, purpose, and clarity. It dissolves blocks and wounds in the womb, reconnecting you with your innate power. Healings of natal and prenatal experiences occur, releasing anger, sadness, grief, and sorrow, all of which are stored in the womb.

This exercise can initate physical cleansing, purging, and the release of toxins and ancient fatigues. Traumas and stresses stored in the cells and nervous system can dissolve quickly. As this deep-seated stress releases, tremors reverberate throughout the nervous system, clearing away the old to bring in the new.

The womb invites our awakening by allowing us to relax, give up, and let go of attachments. As we do so, we come into deeper and deeper states of union, of eliminating the old, and of birthing ourselves. We may go through the densest, darkest parts of ourselves to do this, but rest assured, a new lightness, a new potency, and a new empowerment will be born that is based on your essence as a woman. Deep states of feminine, womb-centered meditation naturally arise through the opening and activation of the womb. This meditation is deep, still, and vast, and centered on your true power source.

Using the womb as a gateway to meditation, as millions of women have done before you, enables you to relax more deeply into your essence, and to explore meditation from a uniquely feminine context. In this form of meditation, you connect with the lineage of ancient mothers— the goddesses and evolved women throughout history, who are there to welcome, support, and guide you back home to your original self.†

---

*To find workshops on Compassionate Womb Breathing, visit the author's website, which is listed in the resource section at the end of this book, and click on Events.
†Some of these women include the Three Marys, Yeshe Tsogyal and the family of Buddha Padmasambhava, the Egyptian Gods or Neters, and many retinues of Buddhist Dakinis and lamas.

The Journey of the Compassionate Womb

The compassionate womb ultimately takes you down deep into the womb of the world, the vast blackness from where all deep transformation arises. Simply by being in this space, you are contributing to the healing of Gaia's and humanity's ills. Many advanced meditators and monks meditate in these spaces to assist humanity as part of their vow to help all beings transcend suffering, and they are available to connect with you also as you travel into this space. It is in the womb of the world that both women and men can go back to the beginning of creation, before the world was formed, simply through the sound codes and breath rhythms that are supported by the lineages of ancient mothers, past, present, and future.

As you access your womb, it gives you a felt sense of nurturing fullness and trust. What we are is held within the Shakti Circuit, and it becomes easier and easier to let go into it the more we feel this flow. In the fully connected Shakti Circuit, the womb gives you the experience of feeling that all is divine, which is the opposite of the patriarchal view that God is "out there" somewhere. As our minds begin to recognize all as divine, our hearts fall in love with it all.

You determine the journey with your intent. If you come only to explore and be of service you will be rewarded with simple efforts and sustained focus. If you come to command into being from the depths of my space, you will be put to the test to reach them. Love, wisdom, and power rule me. You cannot enter without all three. Power to push through the darkness, love flowing out of every breath of intent to the Divine Mother to open the pathway, and the wisdom to know what is called for in each moment. By entering me, you commit to being taught and to learning all three.

This is not just a journey into the womb of the Divine Mother. This is a journey into the self; you cannot access her depths until you look at, realize, forgive, and surrender every aspect of yourself, including the very idea that you have a self. It is a deep, illuminating journey to the heart of life . . . service to all beings . . . and a great honor to tread there. (T.A.)

Love and Power

Journeying into the womb requires the balance and union of love and power. You cannot have union if each quality is only listening to itself. Power listens to love and is informed by love's soft voice, which power serves and honors. Love is informed by power as its fuel to go deeper, beyond the resistance and the layers, to penetrate to the core, where even more love resides in the silence.

The process works both ways in the uniting of heart and womb, power and love, through wisdom. The inherent wisdom of Shakti guides love and power, informing and directing your movements until you become a vehicle for Shakti to move through your bodymind ever deeper. As this happens, the head becomes free and the brain physically relaxes, opening up more space. The actual biological circuitry of the Shakti Circuit activates and opens in a felt physical, emotional, mental and spiritual sense; it is felt on all levels, and in your core.

In the beginning it may be harder to find the power. For others it may be hard to access the sweetness of love. To merge these qualities is a journey in itself. Power needs love and love needs power in order to be whole, but our culture has divorced these qualities. Love has become romanticized, a fairytale or tragic drama, and power has become a force and monstrosity to be feared. To merge love and power, compassion and will, within a female form is even rarer in our world, yet it is the key to our world's freedom.

Going into the womb of compassion I found power. Deep explosions from the belly that electrified my entire being and commanded to be heard. The breath and the sound became a circle within itself, creating and regenerating with every breath. In and out—from womb to heart, from heart to womb—there was a flowing, cyclic, wholeness of energy within myself, and a deep pulsing. But it was all force.

I felt it move into my heart, burying my own tenderness. Strong, potent . . . but without the fullness of love, without vulnerability. It was like a beacon: strong, steady, announcing its light to the night. It could withstand

anything. I felt all this pour into my heart with every burst of power, every
sounding. Feeling, simply feeling was the most beautiful tonic. (W.C.)

The compassionate womb of love and power is a journey of connection and deep, fulfilling empowerment in a visceral manner. It can
connect those who have birthed physical children back to the rhythm
of birth, but in a deeper way: to birth themselves. In this practice, you
connect to your own womb, the gateway to all wombs and the womb
of creation. It is through this connection that a group of women can
connect to the collective womb of humanity, and then to the womb
of the world. It is from this space that deep alchemy can happen, individually and collectively, for all women connect and merge together on
profound, magical, and sacred levels through the womb. It is one of the
most secret and sacred of the Divine Feminine mysteries of Creation.

I sought the rhythmic flow of breath, sound, and body until it found me,
and together we became the vehicle that was aligning with the womb of the
world and the collective. My body became the purging and the birthing.
My mind had surrendered and allowed the organic and familiar unfolding
of this sacred service. My heart and womb were filled with the warmth
of love, compassion and forgiveness, along with strength and power. I felt
held within the womb of the world, as if by a loving sister. (C.O.)

As you deepen into the compassionate womb, your heart flows with
the womb, and then into Source. As all emotions, thoughts, feelings, even
the breath ceases, one connects through the clear and pure heart. Form,
time, and space dissolve into no form, no time, no space, and no mind.

The inside and the outside became one.
W. C. AND CHRIST YESHUA

The in and out breath become the same, the outside and the inside
become the same. Your out-breath becomes God's in-breath, and your

in-breath becomes God's out-breath. Your body and Being is breathed for you, by the Divine.

You become taken over, lost in the spaciousness of creation.

To breathe in God with every breath, to surrender yourself with each exhalation, is a practice in itself. Every breath becomes an embrace, like bodies intertwined, penetrating and being penetrated, dissolving and being dissolved until there is no longer any breather . . . or anyone being breathed. Only breath, love, presence.

When you are lost, Shakti guides you back to your center, which is vast, fathomless, and lovingly powerful. She takes you into the depths of being itself, in a way you have never been before. Breath, love, power, and light combine to take you back into your beginning and end.

In surrender to the instinctual flow of the breath, the lungs empty and move into silence. They begin to fill all on their own, feeling this out-breath of God filling them, and in deep gratitude sending it back out to Him/Her. This is the most beautiful dance of the breath rhythm in its sweetness, fullness, emptiness, and connection. This space is void of pictures, emotions, thoughts, sensations . . . it becomes pure breath, pure essence. Even if the mind enters briefly to feel into the experience with consciousness, it may not perceive anything "happening." And yet, in the multiple dimensions that we exist in, many things are happening. (T.A.)

THE WOMB AND DNA

The Womb holds our DNA patterns, past, present and future. The ancestral DNA patterns within most human beings keep them stuck in the deepest traumas, pain, anger, sadness, and suffering. Genetic patterns are passed on from family to family, ancestor to ancestor. At each step along the way of this long genetic chain, each generation can add qualities or additional defects to the DNA pattern, passing this information down to the next generation, and so on.

For example, the mother of a scientist friend of mine bent and broke her finger in her early twenties. When John was born this manifested in a curled up finger, which then also manifested in his daughter . . . and so on. The cycle continues until one person resolves and heals the trauma on the genetic level, literally becoming a savior or a "Christ" for his or her bloodline.

The Womb holds our DNA patterns, past, present, and future. In the release of family and ancestral imprints, we can go into fever and catharsis as these deep imprints dissolve. Once we truly clear and heal our genetic distortions, our ancestors and descendants also receive the healing.

This is a potent, deeply visceral, physical, emotional, and spiritual experience. It can change the brain and bodymind, and you can feel it deeply in your bones, and in the dissolution of the mind into vast, empty space. This is not something you just receive; you have to give your all to receive it.

In experiencing this mandala with the intention of clearing my DNA ancestral lineage back to the first ancestor, I was graced to feel and understand Christ's experience on the cross. He went through this clearing first on a grand scale for all of humanity. The first to journey so that others may follow always goes through the most difficult tests. I was filled with a comprehensive gratitude of new heights for his conscious gift to us, one that even makes it possible for us to follow his example. In turn, in our giving, we can make the way easier for those that follow us.

In the healing of our own vessel and being willing to take into ourselves all the distortions and sufferings of our ancestors, we create great healing for all of humanity, including our future generations that won't carry these distortions forward any longer. We become the true bridge to bring the essence of God into our physical form.

The experience of all of these ancestors around you, as if they have been waiting to see if you could do it, knowing you were the one born to do so, and giving you support, is deeply moving. Feeling the deep humility of this place, the purity of the healing in process, and the deep connectedness of it all to you as an "individual" and you as all things is profound enough to create the desire to return again and again. (T.A.)

All the mothers in my ancestral lines, back to the first, were present for this clearing. In love, gratitude, and support, they sounded with me, deepening the commitment and presence, which rippled out into the collective, whispering to those ready to hear from within. Spiraling, shimmering strands of ancestral DNA, connecting us all, being cleared and cleansed in the golden infinity loops flowing between the ovaries, from the womb to the heart, between the nipples and from the heart to the third eye. (C.O.)

New Human Being and New DNA

Both the DNA and "junk" or disconnected DNA constantly emanate vibratory signals, pulses, messages, and transmissions throughout your whole bodymind, effectively creating a genetic hologram that then manifests in the 3D world around you. In the 3D collective consciousness the hologram created by the junk DNA signals has come to be known as the "technospheric" matrix—the matrix of technology, human thought, and the collective consciousness of humanity that is based on fear.

The technosphere is the mirror representation of the disconnected DNA patterns. Together the two forms create a virtual mirror net, where the internal manifests the external structures, which in turn keep the mass of humanity bound and hypnotized in the 3D world. These structures feed and live off of negative emotions, bodily dysfunctions, and apparently unshakeable inherited family traumas and behavior patterns.

These distorted structures farm energy from the DNA, on a family and collective consciousness level, guiding it into supporting the ever-expanding technospheric matrix, literally feeding it with human life force so it can grow. The distortions then become even more entrenched in the collective consciousness, feeding back into the human DNA and creating a feedback loop or junk DNA pattern: a vicious cycle.

Together, the junk DNA that contains the codes of self-limitation, and its mirror image in the technospheric matrix create one single entity—the ancient mind of humanity. When we become aware of these distortions and transmute them, we can leave this ancient mind of the mass consciousness behind.

In order for humanity to begin its next phase of evolution, a new species will have to be born on Earth, one that is biologically and genetically different from present-day humanity. In this separation to become whole, what Yeshua called "separating the wheat from the chaff" we actually redeem our bloodlines. In practice this means that our mothers, fathers, daughters, and sons separate genetically from us because our DNA changes.

This is a wonderful thing! I feel more open, more loving, and more joyous with my parents now that this genetic resonance has transformed, and they both feel it too. Both my father and mother noticed the difference in our relationship. My father had lucid dreams (replete with various Masters, which was surprising as he was not really spiritual at this time) about me leaving him and the whole ancestral lineage the night that my DNA changed, without his knowing what was happening to me in another country thousands of miles away. My mother agreed to release me to the Divine Mother, and in a potent ceremony this was done. Then, as physical evidence for us all to notice, this release resulted in a dissolution of her chronic diabetes and all of its attendant symptoms. She also saw herself on a field strewn with corpses. As she stood there amid this carnage, she saw that the corpses were all her family members—brothers, sisters, father, mother, husband . . . all identities now dead. All these corpses were part of herself, and she viscerally recognized that she was now dead to her old self.

DNA and the Lightbody

Our lightbodies carry within them etheric strands of DNA that link them to the physical body, and all the way to Source. The blueprint of each soul is transferred through these etheric strands of DNA, many of which lie dormant in our higher lightbodies. In this way, lightbodies act as the vibratory infrastructure of the DNA.

When the DNA field is cleared and transmuted, it aligns with our unique soul blueprint, and we can then connect directly to God consciousness through the "threads of the One." These strands are cosmic lifelines of vibration and communication that connect us to universal intelligence, the Source. Once connected we literally become as the Maya describe us: "the road to the sky leading to the umbilical cord of the universe."

When the DNA is cleared of ancestral patterns, family behaviors, and the matrix mirror of the technosphere, we enter and access these "threads of the One." In India this is also known as the *sutra atman*—the thread of souls. All souls are strung upon this thread that connects all life forms—humans, birds, animals, even other civilizations in distant parts of the galaxy. This thread is also known as the Tortoise Tube. We are all like beads on this superstring that weaves its way through time and space. We connect to this thread through our open crown and root chakras: the thread just flows through us, and we can follow it with our awareness if we allow ourselves to.

We are all connected on these threads that weave the complex web of life on our planet and throughout time and space. These threads of the One create you, moment to moment, connecting all living beings in an unbroken cord—a cord that is unbroken between you and the birth of awareness itself.

CONSCIOUS BIRTHING

During pregnancy, women have an opportunity to transmute many things. This applies equally to pregnancy with a physical child, a creative project that is a deep part of you and your soul purpose, or the birthing of yourself into happiness. The lessons such a time can dredge up in you include the deepest wounds, pains, and denials you have.

Parental and ancestral issues, family and moral values, fear and guilt, all can rear their head in a conscious pregnancy designed to evolve you, so that you can give birth to a conscious child/project/soul mission.

In consciously birthing a child, we come to understand that the child's soul or body of light is also "born" or brought into matter. During the three stages of labor the baby's lightbody is also being guided and navigated from the darkness of the womb into the world. Traditionally, the father of the baby would guide this process of pure consciousness, while the mother focused more on the physical aspects of birthing. At certain times, both parents come together and merge their lightbodies to form a primordial trinity with the baby. This allows the whole of the baby's soul and different bodies of light to feel safe, supported, and guided to fully enter the body. Today, this rarely, if ever, happens.

During the delicate time of birth, the energies of all three people are involved: The baby relies on the father to meet and guide it to its new home, so that *all* of it can land in the world, and be expressed. The mother relies on the father to support and reassure her through her process of pain and pleasure, and the father relies on the mother being able to push through her labor pains to birth. The baby's foundation on Earth relies totally on mother and father to achieve their union of body, mind, and soul.

This role of the masculine in birthing has been forgotten as consciousness on Earth has declined, yet it is crucial for a conscious birth. The male serves to guide the pure, infinite consciousness of the newborn child into the bodymind so there is an integration of them both. He merges with the new soul and guides the trinity of father, mother, child into being here on Earth. In Egypt, this practice was common among conscious parents who wished to guide their child's soul into the fullness of all it could be. You too can do this now. Whatever you wish to birth you can, provided it is in your highest interest, as a part of your soul purpose, a part of the divine plan.

The current cultural distortions that present birthing as a female-only practice are a result of the gender inequalities on this planet.

Birthing is both men's and women's business, and the more involved men become, the more the baby will benefit. The parents will benefit too, in their emotional and spiritual growth. They will also become closer.

Birthing a baby's soul onto Earth is like helping a soul move through the Bardo—the many veils of living and dying found in the non-physical realms that constitute 94 percent of our universe. These nonphysical realms are protected by many sorts of guardians. These guardians can relinquish their hold on a baby's soul if guided by an expert; if not, these veils can remain in place for many years, and even a lifetime, obscuring a child's full presence in the world. As the baby grows up, he or she can dissolve some of these veils through growth and experience, and he or she may visit a skillful teacher who can help dissolve obscurations.

If this process is done through pregnancy and conscious birth, the process of evolution for baby is far quicker as it grows up. You can save your child many years of suffering by guiding it through the Bardo layers skillfully, allowing the child to attach its lightbody more fully to body and mind. This in itself is the goal of all spiritual traditions that talk about enlightenment: to embody the body of light fully, or become en–light–end. You can give your child a HUGE head start in life by bringing his or her soul into alignment with his or her bodymind from the beginning of life, rather than the middle, the end, or never.

This process begins by communicating with your baby in the womb. Mother and father can talk with baby every day. When you ask the baby questions, you can receive clear answers. Father too can communicate telepathically, and the baby will respond. This process is far clearer once you have cleared and activated your womb, and discovered your womb name. This is part of the reason to attend womb trainings and healings, so birth can be conscious at every stage. Increased consciousness will also prepare the womb to give birth in an orgasmic way, rather than the painful way that has become the norm.

As I have discovered, this communication can be remarkably clear and multidimensional, involving holographic imagery, feelings, and messaging. Baby will let you know exactly what it wants once you start communicating with it, which is initiated by the woman getting to know her womb, her womb name, and healing the wounds that lie there.

Babies respond best to sacred languages like Sanskrit, Aramaic, Tibetan, Egyptian, and various indigenous dialects. This is because sacred languages are not man-made but are rather the sounds of our souls, not interfered with by the middleman of the mind. Babies respond to this most, as it reflects their state of innocence and connection to the Divine, and they can resonate most easily with it. So experiment, and sing/chant to your child or fetus, for all babies respond to one sacred language most strongly.

So, parents: Take the time to get to know your unborn child . . . enter your child's world and learn what is important to that soul. Listen to the lessons you will be learning together; your child has lessons for you as you will have for him or her. For this is the time when the soul is not yet bound by the body, and it can communicate with you with full consciousness. There will never be a more perfect time for you to know the soul of your child, and the fullness of his or her being. Your child will thank you!

The Moon and the Womb

Silver Pathway to the Divine

Water is the body of life force, that moon is its luminous form. As far as the life force extends, so far extends the waters, and so far does the moon extend. These are all equal, and all without limit. One who meditates upon these as finite attains a finite world, whereas one who meditates upon them as infinite attains an infinite world.

BRHADARANAYAKA UPANISHAD

THE MOON IS AN ASPECT of the Silver Ray, the feminine pathway. It is the harmonizer and governor of the womb's ebbs and flows. As the moon waxes and wanes, so does the womb flow with the cycles of life in the oceans. And it is from the oceans that life first sprang forth on this planet.

When the womb harmonizes with the moon's beams—the qualities of the moon in manifestation—then the womb flowers and opens, finding its own voice, its own wisdom, and its own lucid clarity in reflection.

We have forgotten how to honor and work with the moon. As a collective we have forgotten its deeper meaning and purpose. Women have lost touch with their source, and most women do not even know anymore how to align their menses with the natural cycles of the moon.

141

They are instead popping pills and inserting devices into their bodies to make their bleeding more convenient, or simply nonexistent. We are caught up in "getting the job done," getting forward in life, and are ignoring the inner call of the womb that desires to be honored.

Women say they do not have the time to explore and understand their bodies, or to go within and cherish their time of bleeding as a womanly and spiritual experience. Many take painkillers to stop any feeling coming from their wombs. They are in pain because their wombs are crying out for help and healing. The wombs want to be heard. They need to be heard. They deserve to be heard. Why do we keep shutting them up?

Women are still trying to be men, to compete in a man's world. Women have stopped truly honoring their temples, their wombs, their cycles, and the moon, which governs all of these, and our Earth.

The moon's sounds are rarely sung, its virtues rarely extolled. Its qualities of lucidity, clarity, beauty, and universal law have been put to the side in favor of more direct masculine attributes. Its qualities of reflection, however, have been dominating the mindset of humanity, in the form of the bitter wars that happen when reflection becomes projection, unconscious manipulation, and attack.

Humanity has polarized on the dark side of the moon, forgetting its light side, so enmeshed have we become in polarity. The moon is making a resurgence with women to redress this balance, to bring us forward into harmony with the Silver Ray, to ground the feminine path, to remember the moon within our wombs that nurtures, fulfills, and sustains us.

The moon helps us to embrace the often-difficult path that emotions create, to bring us into joy, peace, and clarity. The moon softens and embraces, bringing us back into cyclic flow once more, reestablishing the harmony of the music of the spheres within us. It forges a pathway through emotion, with emotion as the key to movement. With the moon we use feeling as the way to realize truth. The moon brings our feelings to the front, and right in our center; she brings us patience, depth, and the soft power of endurance that no masculine has without her. She brings us soft understanding based on our feeling another, and moving from this feeling in relating. She gently reminds us, the lunar voice deep in our soul, softly whispering.

The moon is the reminder of our connection between the mortal and immortal. She shares a common womb with both; she is the link between human and Divine. This is why she is so important today, for it is only through inclusion of her pathway that humanity can ascend. It is only through embrace, recognition, and loving of all sides of us, light and dark, that we can be all that we are.

When we tune into the moon, we can find a warm and reflective Presence that can share and guide us in many areas. It could be gratitude; it could be her reminding you that she is there for you to use in reflection; to see what is going on with you, emotionally, mentally, spiritually. A man will receive a gentle reflection through tuning in to his heart, listening and seeing what the moon is presenting to him, and what that means for his growth within, not outside himself.

THE QUALITIES OF THE MOON

O rich in brilliance, with your many and varied
illuminations, grant to this singer life giving energy and
wealth, bright, and delightful. O Luminosity, vast with
mighty energies, pour forth thy bright flames to the one
who lauds thee.

HYMN OF CREATION, RK VEDA

The qualities and character of the moon have been forgotten, its names and meanings lost over time. This chapter is based on the 108 Sanskrit mantras to the Moon, detailing her in all her manifestations. Let us pause, and remember these aspects of ourselves for a moment.

The Moon was generated from the mind of god,
The sun generated from the eye of god

The moon came first,
The sun second

The Moon,
Full, whole perfect,
Serenely reflecting the splendor of the sun, the Self,
Makes it accessible to us all

Distilling, purifying, refining us into the silence
    from where awareness springs
Lucid, delighting, refreshing even the most weary of
    souls
A harbinger and a resting place,
Full of contentment, ease, and grace
A safe harbor

Always full,
Always united in its sixteen phases,
Ever present, continually creating, moving in the
    perfect circle of symphonious sound
Ever growing, feeding, and nourishing
The waters, the plants, the herbs, and the flows in
    our bodies and oceans,
The depths of our minds restless in desire
Are stilled thru thy silent reflection,
Cool, serene, the juices of silently swaying colors
The flames of passion, silver slivers of light
Purifying through your cycles and mandalas
Now returning once again

Measuring out creation, measuring out consciousness
Creating the periods of light and dark
The Moon is the cause of time

The fulfiller of desires
The immortal, pure, shining victory
Ever present in the fullness of glory

The nectar that grants all enjoyments,
The taste that quenches all thirsts,
The happiness of all relationships,
The juices found in the flow of joy,
The dissolver of the poverty of suffering,
The protector of the soul

Arising from the ocean of consciousness
You reflect being as it moves into manifestation
An ocean of compassion,
Soft and silvery,
Moonbeams and slivers of light illuminating hidden
      mysteries
Realized through our devotion

The protector of the world
The remover of suffering
Worshipped by the wise
Worshipped by the twice born
Those who have died into true Self
With white body and golden ornaments
Wearing garlands of white flowers
Bright formed like jasmine

Borne of the waters
Holding the scepter, the flow of holy law
Ever unchanging, serene and still in continual
      reflection
The giver of the Beloved

The flow of love that soothes all beings
Ocean of compassion
Tranquil, pure, and serene
Always there, always here
Reflected in the acts of our own hearts
Reflected in our relations with others
Reflected in the stillness of our minds
The reflection of self to self in the eye of One Self

I Am the affection between lovers
I Am the lovers' friend
Flooded with the juices of creating ever flowing
Restless with desire, ever forming and unfolding
I am the self-confidence, respect, and honor you give
  your true Self
The first steps to manifestation

I stand firm in consciousness, ever maintaining my
  position
Flowing throughout all creation
No identity yet all identities
I am the mark by which you measure yourself
I am the step you must take
I am the word you have yet to utter
I am the fullness that contains all.
                          PADMA AON PRAKASHA

BREATHING WITH THE MOON

Now that we have remembered more about the essence of the moon, we can begin to actively work with this splendid, gracious, and loving being that refreshes, delights, and clarifies us. We can do this by breathing the moon into the womb, and by sounding the names, sounds, and mantras of the moon, as women have done for thousands of years before us in the lineages of ancient mothers and grandmothers, throughout history. Every woman is connected to this lineage of birthing and the moon; it simply has to be remembered within you.

Breathing the moon into the womb happens through the kidneys. The kidneys are the feminine energy chi generators of the body. The energy they generate is sky-blue in nature and is pure clarity in essence. When they are stimulated they send feminine chi to all parts of the body, especially to those areas that need it.* Kidney chi is refined, energizing, and healing, and with intent it can be used to energize the womb and connect it to the moon through the feminine Silver Ray of light.

In this practice the kidneys become the conduit for the Silver Ray of the moon (the lunar path of the feminine), bringing lunar light into the body's energy pathways and meridian circulatory system. The Silver Ray refines and purifies, clearing fogginess and lack of clarity, re-evoking the memories of water, chi, and the feminine, balancing the excess masculine back into harmony. It activates those areas of the body that need the feminine energy, that have become stagnant and disused.

If you feel disconnection to the true feminine, or feel tightness at the heart, this practice can assist you in harmonizing emotions, making you more patient, balanced, and persevering. If done regularly, kidney and womb connection leads to a more flowing, cooling, gentle and mothering energy within you, balancing excess mental attitudes and expressions. This practice can also be used to vivify and energize you, as it was used by Egyptian healers as a means of charging up the kidneys so they could have more power to heal others.

---

*To work with the kidneys, please see the Kidney Breathing exercise on page 43.

Weaving Shakti Deeper

The Shakti Weave, Shakti Breathing, and Ovary Breathing

If we look at the body of the perfect human, the full expression of joy lies in the completely opened root chakra. The full expression of limitless co-creation lies in the completely opened sacral chakra. The full expression of selfless power lies in the solar plexus chakra. The full expression of love lies in the heart chakra. The full surrender and expression of divine creation, or the Word, is held in the throat chakra. The full seeing and perceiving, the full penetrating of all veils and illusions, the single eye, the eye that sees all, is held in the third eye chakra. The formless light that is flawless and perfected is held in the crown chakra.

Meditate on these qualities within. Ask yourself if you have fully experienced these qualities. If you cannot sustain these qualities, look at what is hampering and blocking you.

Let me elaborate: the joy in the root chakra is not just felt in the root. It is felt in the totality of the whole being. It is physical but not physical. It comes from the root but is felt all over, encompassing and enveloping the whole being in joy. The limitless co-creativity in the sacral chakra is the ability to manifest and co-create the divine plan on Earth. This limitless co-creation is fully activated between man and woman through the eighteen pathways of the Shakti Circuit.

The selfless power in the solar plexus comes when there is no more grasping, need, or attachment to the idea of an individual self. To be selfless requires great power, otherwise one leaks energy, and becomes weak. This solar power is fed and nurtured through delight and giving.

The heart of unconditional love is honest, humble, giving, and seeing the perfection in all life. The grace to sink deep into your nature, this is the most natural thing of all. All you can do is remove the layers and barriers to this, and allow it to issue forth in its own way, in its own time. At the throat chakra is where we surrender and allow our bodyminds to be used as an expression of Source, of the Word.

As the throat manifests divine eloquence or divine expression, you reach a state where each thought, word, and deed manifests as one. This is part of the meaning of confession. Confession allows discrepancies among thoughts, words, and deeds to be dissolved, so you can return to your original blueprint where thought, word and deed are one. In order to reach this divine expression and surrender, you have to be humble and confess your faults and shortcomings, and forgive them.

With an open third eye you have the eyes to see; with an open throat you have the ears to hear. Seeing is a direct experience of oneness. It is a clear knowledge of the divine plan, allied with the ability to organize, co-create, and manifest it on Earth.

THE SHAKTI WEAVE

Now that we have seen the body of the perfect human, let us turn our attention to the body of woman, holder of the mysteries of the universe. Fewer women have become fully enlightened throughout history because they have forgotten the workings of their own biology and their own wombs, and they are being led by men who also do not know these truths. The feminine pathway to full empowerment has its own ways, even though the destination is the same for women as it is for men.

In women, the opening of the third eye has to come from both the back of the brain—the lunar entrance to the third eye known as the Alta Major—and the front of the brain—the pineal gland, or solar entrance to the third eye, along with with the rest of the Shakti Circuit.

The openings at the back of the brain can be felt, and accelerated into, by two partners working together sitting back to back, with the backs of their heads touching. This creates standing waves of Shakti that move up and down the spine, connecting Shakti energy through infinity loops. This is known today as the Shakti Weave.

The re-awakening of Shakti is accelerated and amplified in the mandala of the Shakti Weaving, the dance between two. I am the giving, the life force of creation. When allowed clear channels in which to flow, I transmute fear to love. I am the emptying. I am the filling. Ride this circuit with loving presence. Let it become your breath. The dance, the beautiful dance of my weaving . . . moving in, out, through, around in endless loops of infinity is the power to connect with oneself, with another, with God at such a level

The Shakti Weave

that you can realize and receive simultaneously the service of giving—the essence of the soul's reason for being.

[I am] wild. I have no mind; I have no form. Leave thought behind— leave any attempts to grasp at and define my limitless being. I am unfathomable. The present moment is my portal, and my playground. Feel. Feel me now. The sparking of life and creation bubbling forth from within you. Up out of your root, out of the earth, out of the fire of your being. In the meeting of breath, in the meeting of bodies, in this divine union I take form. In relation, in service, in transcendence, in giving: you give me life. Ignite me. I exist to give, to move, and to transform.

I AM life. I AM the body of creation in all its forms. Pure energy. Pure being overflowing in the constant dance of becoming. Breathe me in and I will breathe into the forgotten pieces of yourself . . . softly, sweetly, fiercely giving life to their frostbitten form. Trust me, fall into me, move with me, drink me in and breathe me back out into the source from which I come—and into your partner—with love, gratitude, and surrender. I am beyond any concept of self. I will flow through, and break through, any resistance to life. To other. To living. To now. To embracing the full present body of your being. (A.R.)

There is a dance, a flow of experience when two come together and breathe in the Shakti Weave. There can also be great healing, for when Shakti is fully present and engaged, the transmutation of dense, stuck energies occurs naturally. For the partners engaged in the Shakti Weaving, there is a great experience of bliss. Anger, frustration, and similar thought forms arising from the cells only give Shakti more fuel for bliss, more fuel to transmute. The harder and faster they arise, the more bliss is manifested in the body, until these forms dissolve and the dance returns to the soft flow of two bodies swaying in sync to Shakti's rhythm; spine to spine, like a snake undulating rhythmically to a flute.

In this state of bliss you are in total service—in two ways. One is through simply being in the flow of the delicious dance of the Shakti Weave with your partner. The second is in allowing yourself to move into deeper levels of presence, allowing energies to come through you—from both your and your partner—which can then be carried on Shakti's flow and embraced, transmuted, and dissolved.

Shakti is really all about giving—womb to womb, or womb to hara. You open up and surrender your soul without limits, without wanting for self or needing to gain anything for self. Here there is no self. The soul surrenders its identity without expectation into the flow of Shakti, and dissolves into pure spirit. The bodymind becomes its vehicle.

You surrender to the flow within, and surrender to letting it flow out of you, without the expectation of receiving it back. Regardless of who this energy is flowing to, they will be touched, for the flow of Shakti into a man or woman sharing the Weaving with you will of course be a great spark of ignition.

There is an even deeper level to which this can be taken, and that is to pull Shakti up into the heart creating layers of infinity loops. There is one loop between your two ovaries or testes, there is another between your heart and womb, and still another ignites as these two loops pull their focus to the heart and connect to each other.

This practice really needs no conscious intent, as it is the natural flow of Shakti from the heart to emanate in all directions, especially to another heart. This creates openings to the crystalline grids in the body, and a realignment of your true DNA structure. You may notice interesting physical effects in your body and brain as you allow higher vibrations to continually enter and recalibrate you.

SHAKTI BREATHING

I bubble forth; I am the wellspring. I carry in my essence the realization that you are God in every cell of your being. As I flow in and through you, each cell becomes enlivened, each cell bursts with life, with joy at this arrival for now it can live and breathe even without oxygen for its true source of replenishment has been reconnected. As I flow, the dance of life begins. The body pulses and sways from within in an eternal dance of

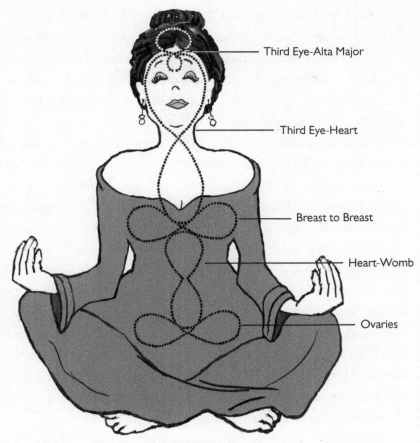

Third Eye-Alta Major

Third Eye-Heart

Breast to Breast

Heart-Womb

Ovaries

The infinity loops of Shakti

constant creation; perpetual motion in alignment with every part of the universe. The dance once begun can never cease—indeed it never has.

Let the Pulse move through you and out into the world with every breath. Rather than breathing in from the world looking for sustenance; continually breathe out—perpetually breathing out from God to all of humanity. Dance with me and with every other part of creation for they are all flowing with my essence, with the essence of God—just waiting for you to acknowledge it and dance with them. The Sun, the moon, the flowers, the trees, the waters, the creatures of land, sea and sky—all flow with me, and want to dance the joy of life with you. (C.O.)

The life force is breath. Without breath, there is no life. The rhythms of our breath connect us to the breath of the Divine that is Shakti. When united, the breaths run throughout your body and mind as a wave moves through an ocean, changing and connecting all it touches. As we inhale, spiraling rhythms of breath radiate outward from every cell and atom—as we exhale, we spiral inward.

With every breath we breathe in 10^{23} atoms—a thousand trillion trillion of them—which join us to become part of us; we then breathe out a similar number of atoms that were part of our bodies just a moment before. Our bodyminds, through the breath, are in this constant state of transformation, exchanging life force with the rest of the universe all the time. We literally are breathing Obama's and Christ's air!

It is through the breath that we build a bridge between conscious and subconscious, releasing stress, old memories, beliefs, emotions, and reactive tendencies by pumping more life force to all parts of the body and mind, giving us more energy to engage with life. It has been said that if we were to change nothing except our breathing (not our eating, exercise, thinking patterns, or habits), we could radically alter our lives. The paradox is that as soon as we do change the breathing pattern, all the other things change as well.

Breathing deeply into the eighteen pathways of the Shakti Circuit creates a regenerating, nourishing continuum of life flow that feeds body, mind, and soul. This energy is then directed into the ruby red ovaries to charge them up, to charge up your bodymind with light. The ovaries are the light and sexual energy generators of your body. To charge them directly from your deepest womb space allows them to become reconnected, to become active agents of your womb's love and deepest desires, to become agents of your soul's mission and purpose on Earth.

As this energy connects with the infinite heart loop, softly and slowly, you ground your light and power into the dance of the heart. As you rise into the diamond of your third eye, you can command all this generated energy to open and activate, one seed at a time, the potentials that are held within your womb. This is holy desire merging with open, flowing Shakti power—the union of love, feminine power, and womb wisdom, through the breath of life. It is in this space—where you are connected to your womb, heart, and third eye—that you can begin to manifest your dreams in reality.

Each time your Circuit is infused with energy through the breath, you experience a higher expansion of the level of light you can hold in your physical body. This results in the reconstruction of your cellular makeup. The cells, rather than being oval or spherical, begin to take on a more diamond-like shape, a higher geometric patterning that heightens their interconnectivity, and therefore their ability to carry information and light.

Every cell becomes a portal. Corrections and adjustments occur in the electrical fields that have been out of attunement, and the whole body benefits from realignment within the organs. Each cell begins to clear long-held obstacles, and more energy, authority, and centeredness arise within you as a result.

When you surrender to the breath and can let it breathe you, magic happens. An expansive energy previously unimaginable to you can race in like a charging horse, blasting through residue and firing new sections of the bodymind and brain as the circuit completes. This results in feeling like bursting or literally being "blasted." Senses are heightened to a new, disorienting level that will take the rest of the body some time to catch up to. (T.A.)

THE OVARIES

The rich wine-red ovaries are a storage center for vast amounts of sexual energy, and also a repository of sexual traumas and repression. As the ovaries heal, life force flows into the belly and womb, which can then be directed into other parts of the bodymind via the eighteen pathways to renew, vitalize, empower, and enhance your innate femininity.

More than 40 percent of a woman's daily energy goes into the production of her eggs. Thus a woman loses her vital, sexual energy through her ovaries in the same way that a man loses energy when he ejaculates. If this energy is harnessed through ovary breathing, all this life force can be circulated to improve the health of the body, skin, and organs, increasing your life span, clearing your mind, and boosting your immune system. Ovary breathing is also a great way to open up to having full-body orgasms.

As you deepen in the practice of ovary breathing, many premenstrual stresses and tensions can disappear, and mood swings harmonize. This is because you now have the ability to channel ovary energy anywhere in the eighteen pathways.

Women who master their bodies and harness the energy of their ovaries have the ability to choose whether to become pregnant. The energy pool in the ovaries can be used to rapidly increase fertility and achieve pregnancy, or this energy can be sent to other parts of the body to manifest a different kind of project or creation. This is the natural birth control method that actually makes you feel better!

When the energy from the ovaries is circulated through the eighteen natural energy flows of the female body, it connects the womb, heart, and ovaries to create circuits of light. Life force is converted into light force. This increases a woman's innate abilities to heal and nurture. As this occurs, you discover that the seeds of your creation, with all its potential, are held in this supportive container in order to be able to bloom fully.

In Tibet, the ovaries are seen as containing blueprints for the bloodline, and holding keys for healing the ancestral lineages. The ovaries are also seen as the biological light generators of feminine form, a warehouse of divine potential. The left ovary is silver and the right ovary is ruby. Between them, they create living spheres of energy that activate fully through the fire of love that is generated between a man and a woman. Potentiality thus fertilized can be carried to the womb for gestation and birth.

The ovaries act as guardians, the decisive voice in the call to spark each seed of potential into life. Knowing the alchemical needs of each seed potential, the ovaries have the power to draw in the energetic fire needed to activate each particular seed. They function in this way like a magnet or gatherer to suit a seed's divine purpose. They also hold the capacity to destroy those seeds ignited with false aim.

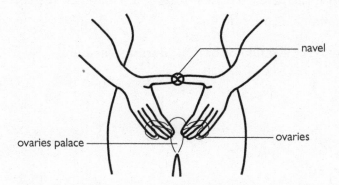

Ovary Breathing is a practice from the Taoist tradition.

🐾 Ovary Breathing

1. Focus on the ovaries in Yoni Mudra, hands forming a downward triangle over the ovaries.
2. Sit quietly, and do throat breathing, rasping the breath over the throat, making an ocean-like sound, with your tongue resting on your palate.
3. Focus on the ovaries until you feel their energy expand and become warm.
4. As you breathe in, gently contract the opening to the yoni, using the muscles of the first gate, and as you breathe out relax the muscles. Use your mind, breath, and muscles to do this gently. Soon you will not need to use the muscles, and the breath and mind will do it automatically. This motion helps to draw energy into the ovarian palace, warming you up.
5. Continue this, and begin to collect the warm energy at the ovarian palace.

6. As this energy builds, you can start to breathe and circulate it into the ovary loop, then the heart loop.

7. You can also send it to the perineum, yoni, and through the gateways, one by one, with the prayers for each gateway: praise, gratitude, and compassion.

8. Finish the practice with storing and sending all the energy into the womb or ovary loops.

This practice should not be done during ovulation.

Umbilical Cords of Connection

Our First Connection, Our First Separation

THE PLACENTA SUSTAINS AND NURTURES you within the womb until you are ready to step out and be born into this world. Placenta and baby both arise from the very same cell, the fertilized ovum, and in a sense that makes the baby and the placenta one, sharing the same etheric field.

The placenta is the first mother to each of us. It is our first connection, our first relationship to this world, our first nourisher, supporter, and companion. It feeds us and offers us all we need to grow. Our sustainer and protector, the placenta provides us with our first experience of unconditional love: it is our first love. When we are cut off from this first source of love prematurely, it leads us to seek love outside of our own selves.

Sadly, this is what happens to almost all of us when the umbilical cord is cut, because we are separated too soon from the life force and soul connection that still pulse through the cord. This cut happens before the placenta has transferred its immune-boosting physical essence, emotional nurturing qualities, and soul essence to us, and this sudden separation creates shock and fear.

Before the moment of cutting, the placenta, womb, baby, and mother are one. When the cord is cut, we actually experience separation for the first time in the bodymind. The loss, abandonment, and grief that we can experience in our unformed bodies and minds as we enter this world, brutally and prematurely cut off from the nurturing, unconditionally loving envelope of the placenta, is a huge conditioning for us.

As an adult, you can heal this separation within yourself through a placenta healing, the power of which hundreds of men and women who have experienced it can testify to. Indeed, this chapter is based on the experiences that many of these men and women have had with the placenta healing method, which reconnects the umbilical cord back to its Source. This healing was originally used by the priestesses of Isis in Egypt, and has been given again to humanity by this lineage in order to accelerate reconnection to the Source within.*

The effects of this healing can be both "wonderful and frightening," as D.K. reports. For him, it felt

> at first as if I was in the womb, surrounded by peace and love . . . a time before any thought. Then I experienced being born. The umbilical cord was cut and I experienced much fear and terror. I felt separate. I had a hard time catching my breath. Finally I was able to breathe through the fear and terror. Then again I felt the peace and love surrounding me, except this time it came from within, and not from without.

The bodymind and soul can really feel how big this trauma is, for when we feel cut off from the umbilical cord, we feel cut off from the information of love.

> I feel my placenta is my own connection to the love of the universe, and a divine connection to other human beings. It's my first connection to universal, unconditional love. When the placenta is cut off too early, one woman experienced "a deep loneliness, sadness, emptiness, and loss. (M.C.)

---

*For information on where to obtain a placenta healing, see the resource section at the end of this book.

When you are cut off from the feeling of love so early in life, many beliefs arise to fill this hole. For some people who have experienced the healing of their placenta, some of the beliefs they formed at the beginning of their lives included feelings of abandonment. One participant reported of her healing experience,

I could be abandoned every time I'm in relation [so] I feel I have put on many subterfuges to not be abandoned.

An inner battle arises between self-love and self-hatred. As R.M. put it,

The following day I literally fell in love with myself! It was a very new feeling to me. . . . I don't know how to explain it but I felt there wasn't a separation anymore between me and myself. I used to feel a little disconnected with who I am, maybe not really accepting who I am. I felt I was back into myself. I wasn't harsh to myself anymore. . . . I was kind to myself.

The healing of this separation can re-evoke in us the cellular memory of being connected, of being nurtured by the Divine Mother. This memory can regift us with a feeling of security about life, our own loving and nurturing capacities, and intimate relationships. Feelings of warmth, kindness, and gentleness return to this part of ourselves that has been forgotten and unnurtured.

As M.C. put it,

The energy that pulses through the cord from the placenta is the Divine Mother nourishing us. It is neither wholly our biological mother's nor ours alone, but something that connects us to one another and to the Divine Mother. This divine energy is transferred to us, into our bodies by the mother through the placenta. Regardless of how our biological mothers feel or who they are, the Divine wants us to thrive more than anything.

The energy we receive while in the womb is what brings Spirit into us.
It is the part that can save us from destroying everything . . . . It is possibly
as close as we can get to Spirit before our souls are fully awakened. It is, in
effect, a great mystery and miracle. The Divine Mother is in and around
all of us—we all have the most wonderful mother, as loving as we can
imagine and beyond.

Letting the placenta drop off and release by itself—usually between
three and seven days after birth—leads to peace and the wisdom, "I
receive," "I have everything I need," and "everything is here, and now."
As another woman put it, "I'm connected to unconditional love of the
source and nothing, never could cut that. I feel myself in security: I'm
loved!"

GAIA'S CORD

In Cambodia the placenta is known as "the globe of the origin of the
soul" and for the Maori it is *te whenua*—the land, which nourishes the
people just as the physical earth does. Mother, child, and land are all
intimately interconnected from the moment of conception itself, each
nourishing and sustaining the others. When one is looked after, the others benefit also. This living connection establishes and sustains the vital
personal and soul link between the land and the child, and between
human soul, physical body, and life force.

When this connection is not honored, life itself is not respected,
and mother, child, and land all suffer. A more conscious way of honoring the connection between placenta and child includes not cutting the
cord, and letting the placenta fall off naturally. It can later be buried
underground, while the mother connects to the land through ceremony.
By these practices, the living threads of energy that interconnect and
sustain us, our communities, and our planet Gaia, are woven together
in a web of life and love.

In healing the umbilicus trauma, we can trigger our body's cellular memory and reconnect with the cord of love that roots us in Gaia. As S.M. shares,

> My body was heavy . . . going into the earth. As I sat with this energy I was visited by three indigenous souls—the longer I sat quietly, the deeper the stillness, the deeper the peace, and the more connected into body and earth I became . . . very nurturing and blessed.

Twin Souls

In many sacred traditions the placenta is seen as a twin soul, or double. The Baganda of Uganda believe that the placenta is actually the child's double, which has its own soul that resides in the umbilical cord. Ancient Egyptian pharaohs believed one soul inhabited the body, while another inhabited the placenta. It was the job of this placental soul to act as the child's guardian from birth; the placenta was thus a valued part of each child, not separate, or useless. In the Old Testament the placenta was thought to be the external soul.

The placenta gives us our first experience on the Earth plane of a twin soul. When the trauma of separation from it is healed we can find this connection within ourselves, rather than feeling compelled to find it outside. We find that we can be for ourselves a source of nourishment and deep inner peace.

RECONNECTING THE CORD

Deep emotion and tears are common during and after an umbilicus healing, as are physical discharges from the womb, fatigue, fever from the healing, headaches, womb cramping, and physical pains and stiffness. This is because the severing of the cord creates a false body attitude in all of us. When the energetic cause of this false attitude is removed, the body can return to its natural state of wholeness. These symptoms arise because of this split between body and mind and are healed by the reintroduction of the soft, enveloping feeling of the placenta's nurturing energy being remembered on the physical level, which creates shifts in conjunction with the body's innate wisdom. As H.T. put it,

I feel I'm making peace with my physical body.

After a placenta healing, many people feel a new and great sense of wellness encoded in their bodies. Expanded states of peace also arise, bringing a feeling that something has finally come to rest deep within: the cord that was cut has now been reconnected back to its source.

It was as if my whole inner being, my self, was gone, joining the deepest part one can search for and being welcome there. This very soft and wonderful vibration traveled all over my body . . . there were no boundaries, just intense light. (J.H.)

L.P. described the energy she experienced as

very soft, flowing very sweet, gentle but powerful, and cleared out a lot of samskaras.

As C.O. recounts,

It felt as my womb felt after giving birth, as an emptying without the intense contractions, a warmth of the flow of something, similar to the bleeding in menses. In my emotional body there was the sense of letting go of something that has been with me my entire physical life.

Remembering this essence on a cellular level is like a

deep basking in the inner light—very sweet. I am becoming significantly less engaged with external drama . . . getting triggered by the world around me far less. I am experiencing lovely feelings of contentment and a sense of being supported by my own Source—the inner light feels near and accessible. I also seem to have had a breakthrough in terms of my tendencies to judge those around me. (D.W.)

Recurrent feelings of shame, self-judgment, and self-worthlessness are simply gone. I do not react to triggers with an automatic response anymore. (U.C.)

The placenta healing can aid the psychosomatic healing of family and ancestral issues that tend to linger on into our adult lives. For U.C., who had done a lot of healing around her mother issues but was unable to break through her inherited family dysfunctions,

healing the placenta also means healing the information that was passed from mother to child in utero. The relief I now feel from this healing is indescribable. I feel that I can now move on and get out in the world in action . . . so that feels like being born, quite simply.

In many births the balance between the energetic and the physical is disrupted by the removal of the placenta while the energetic cords continue to hold connection to the child's soul. In order to complete this unfinished part of the process of whole birth, we have to heal the energetic placenta, reconnect the cord, and then let go of it consciously. Bringing resolution to the spirit-placenta disconnection means that both the child's soul and the mother's soul are free to rest, restore, and regenerate Shakti.

You can remedy the placenta disconnection through gentle natural birth practices for your own children. When allowance is given for the umbilical cord to drop away naturally after birth, all the life force of the placenta gets transferred along the cord to the baby, and the etheric field around baby and placenta is sealed off properly. This complete field results in a stronger immune system and a baby who feels safe, loved, nurtured, respected, and balanced. Such a child is ready to make the step into this world in a secure way that suits its own rhythms.

By honoring the placenta, you can help your children avoid a life programmed by the fears of scarcity, loss, and insecurity that so many of us have experienced. According to anecdotal evidence from midwives used to Lotus Births, such as the births shared in the book *Sacred Birthing* by Sunni Karil, children who have not had their umbilical cord cut prematurely are more peaceful, less disruptive, and better behaved.

The Galactic Center

Returning to the Womb in 2012

I feel my placenta is my own, prototypal connection to the love of the universe, and to a divine connection to other human beings. It's my first connection to universal, unconditional love. (M.P.)

CORDS CONNECT US ALL, FROM the first cord between the mother and her baby to the cords between the chakras, the cords of relationship that connect us to other people, and the cords that connect us to the earth. These cords, also known as leylines or dragon lines, keep the routes of communication alive between us and Gaia, acting as an acupuncture network that crisscrosses the planet.

In the last eons on Earth, many of these cords of relationship and connective pathways have been damaged or severed because of our separation from the placenta and the womb, which acts as our instinctual, primordial connection to Gaia. This severing of cords between the womb and Earth also affects the cords connecting Earth and the Galaxy.

This severing of cords has occurred because of the imbalance between matriarchy and patriarchy, as well as other cataclysmic events that have happened in Earth's history (recorded in the collective memory banks of humanity). These events have ruptured the primordial connection to the womb and the leylines connecting us to Earth, and our galaxy. These cords or leylines connect our wombs/haras to Earth, and then through the web of life to the moon, the planets, and the Milky Way galaxy.

At the center of our Milky Way galaxy lies a massive black hole. The size of our galaxy—and of other galaxies—is inextricably intertwined with the size of this black hole; the bigger the hole, the bigger the galaxy. Scientists and cosmologists are now saying that black holes birthed our galaxy, and possibly even our universe.

This womb center of our galaxy emanates out umbilical cords—resembling the spiraling structure of DNA—which nourish and connect all within the system, just as umbilical cords from the placentas of our mothers connected to us. These cords connect us all to the black hole at the center of our galaxy—the Galactic Womb. Astronomers discovered this black hole in 2002, yet its presence, importance, and connection to Source have been known to the Mayans, Indians, and Egyptians for many thousands of years.

The Mayans call this cord of connection the Kuxan Suum, a lifeline of vibration and communication connecting us from our navels through

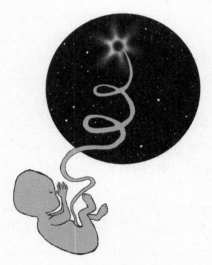

Cord to the Galactic Womb

a spiraling energetic umbilical cord to the Galactic Center, the womb of creation. This connection is set to more fully align to Earth by 2012, the end of time according to the Tzolkin—the Mayan calendar.

In India this umbilical cord or Tortoise Tube connects the God Vishnu through his lotus-shaped navel into the *Padmanabhi,* the lotus center or Galactic Center, where he dreams creation into being. In Egypt the God Khonsu acts as the umbilical cord to the Galactic Center, which is known in that culture as the all-powerful "hidden" God Amun, the God of the most powerful priesthood in Egypt.

All these traditions actively tapped into the Galactic Center through ceremony and ritual that were known to the leaders and priests of their societies. A select few shamanic seers, high priestesses and kings were initiated into these mysteries so they could ride the Kuxan Suum to the Galactic Center. Through the Galactic Center, they could then enter other dimensions, travel to other worlds, and access secret and sacred knowledge about the mysteries of life and death. This was all done for the benefit of their societies, to keep them in alignment with the Divine Mother and the center of creation.

All cords start at this place, our first connection and our first separation. Cords connect us all, human to human, human to Gaia and the galaxy, and beyond. When we truly start to heal and reconnect these cords, and follow them all the way to the Galactic Center, we can realize we are all interconnected, living in the same web of life. Like D.K., we can experience "being in different bodies alive today. We were what appeared to be separate, but all the same. We were all One. In truth it was a feeling of not being able to escape myself. Whatever body I went to, there I was."

THE WOMB, THE PLACENTA, AND THE GALACTIC CENTER

The womb and the hara are our direct connection points to the Galactic Center and beyond. Each individual womb or hara is the gateway into this space and spaciousness. The Galactic Center is not outside of us: it is within the dreaming space of our hearts and wombs united. Each person has this connection within, and each person can activate it.

The Galactic Center and its transmissions are not accessed through the mind, but rather through your primordial creative center in unison with the mind, guided by the womb, which serves as a transmitting agent or servant. Today the possibility exists for all of humanity to access this core of wisdom, love, and power directly—without intermediary. Once the connection is established it is always there. Yet to access this requires healing of all the severed and damaged cords, and then a reconnecting and remembering.

The Galactic Center is the source of this galaxy, the place from which this galaxy was birthed. Where the galactic Equator crosses the ecliptic (the apparent line of the Sun's annual motion relative to the stars), Sagittarius points directly towards the Galactic Center. To observers on Earth, this appears as a dark road that begins near the ecliptic and stretches along the Milky Way. Mayan creation myths describe creation taking place at this celestial crossroads, called the road to Xibalba, the underworld, or the "Black Road." Through this entrance to the underworld road one can travel up to the heart of sky, the Galactic Center.

In 2012 the Galactic Center will be at 27° Sagittarius. At this time the foot of the figure in the constellation Ophiuchus (the Serpent Bearer) will be in conjunction with the Galactic Center, as will the Sun. In the ancient Mayan village of Santiago Atitlan, the villagers call their sacred site *umuxux kaj, u muxux ulep* (navel of the sky, navel of the earth), the place where all creation began at the center of the galaxy. To this day, women there wear headdresses they call the rainbow serpent, a representation of the serpentine umbilical cord connecting each person with Source in the heavens.*

---

*Allen J. Christenson, "Precolumbian Antecedents for Modern Highland Mayan Ceremonialism" in *Iconomania: studies in visual culture* (http://www.humnet.ucla.edu/humnet/arthist/Icono/Christenson/maya.htm), 1998.

The serpent has great importance to the Mayans as a symbol of Shakti, DNA, and the waves of resonance connecting one thing to another. The serpent is also a symbol of the umbilical cord, the connection with the placenta and mother.

Much of the religious ceremony of the Mayans in the later period of their history involved violent sacrifice as well as self-mutilation. These violent tendencies arose, just as they do with all humans, from the trauma of placental cutting. This trauma creates a gaping hole in our psyches—a pattern of more self-violence and harm, and a deep need to compensate for this first loss of love. This need runs throughout our entire lives, and manifests in our need to consume and acquire things, and to exert control over others.

We all adjust to this loss in some way. The degree to which we adjust determines our sense of self-security and well-being. If we do not adjust well, we feel insecurity and neediness; if we adjust well we cover this loss through various masks. It is this sense of loss that motivates us to seek love from the mother—including the mother/womb/placenta at the Galactic Center.

This Galactic womb is where all humans have come from, where we have birthed from, and the place to which we shall all return. It is a source of unconditional love wed with power in an unlimited state, the beginning and the end, the return back to your Original Self. It is the river and flow of Shakti, which connects and unifies all parts of yourself. Much wisdom for humanity lies in the Galactic Center, and it is readily accessed through our primordial creative connection: love, joy, and power united, or womb/hara and heart united.

This is not a transcendent teaching, out there in the cosmos somewhere. Being human and divine without separation is what is being asked of us. The wisdom and loving power contained in the Galactic Center is rapidly accelerating our evolutionary process, as it reconnects us to our first breath, our first cell, the first cellular division that occurs when one becomes two. The Galactic Center is the home of your soul, where male and female are in union, held in an infinite space of fertile possibility, rich in any potential. It is the highest Tantra and union.

Anything can be created here and through the womb/hara, co-creation in this space is possible, and indeed has been done many times in our past. It is the home of your wildest dreams come true once aligned to the natural, innate heart impulse of giving, and your passionate connection to the joyous life force: Shakti.

The Galactic Center is a vast yet intimate space, peaceful but incredibly creative and ever changing. It is the ground of being, still and silent, yet containing the surging exciting bliss and power of creativity within itself. Most people who experience their reunion with the Galactic Center describe it as unconditionally loving, accepting, and supporting of every part of themselves. In this sense it is our mother, the Galactic Womb that nourishes us. The return of this energy now, set to culminate and fully align in 2012, is also the return of the Mother in all her glory. It is the homecoming.

As we journey deeper into the Galactic Center we realize that we are simultaneously creator and co-creation. You can experience yourself creating the world over and over again, watching humanity create itself over and over again throughout the different epochs of history. This is a living experience that is accessed through the Shakti Circuit retreats, when you are ready to co-create with the wisdom of the womb within.* It is here we realize our power as creators, and it is here that we will manifest it in ways that are unimaginable now. For the Galactic Center is the breath of God, inside and out, and it leads us to the pool of infinite creativity that we live in every day, as we create everything moment by moment.

Your heart and your womb/hara are the gateway to the Galactic Center. It is you, and you are it. It is the black in the heart of light, and the blinding illumination found in the deepest recesses. It is here that

---

*See the resource section at the end of this book for more information on Shakti Circuit retreats.

all grids and reconnections to the web of life are grounded, and it is here that our ultimate reconnection lies.

Within the Galactic Center lies the potential for healing all our ancestral lines and for remodeling our DNA to form a new type of human being. In the actual experience of immersing in the Galactic Center, we can become annihilated. A black hole literally absorbs all the light that comes into it, bringing you into Black Light. All parts of you that are still attached will arise to be seen, and the immense love here will break down your constructs. When you are ready to immerse all of yourself into the Galactic Center, you will find that even your hard-won soul awareness has to be given up. You have to give up, and surrender, your soul, to that which lies beyond it.

To enter this space with every part of yourself means the annihilation of ego and soul, and the consequent resurrection of your Self. This death and resurrection will be an octave higher than what you had before. Whereas before your ego died to be reborn with the soul as its master, here the soul surrenders, dying a death so it can be mastered by God. Now it is God moving through you, with the soul as servant.

Many highly evolved beings and stellar intelligences of great light live near the emanations of the Galactic Center. Some of them can withstand the high pressure and intensity of these frequencies, then modulate and share their energy with humanity in forms that we can handle and safely absorb. Some of these waves emanating from the Galactic Center are surfacing as new healing modalities, such as Ilhanoor, Reconnective Healing, and other forms of direct energy transmission.

According to the Mayan calendar, the Galactic Center will be in direct alignment with Earth in 2012, a configuration that will initiate a new phase of evolution for humanity. Practically speaking, this will mean that we can all potentially access and enter a state of superconsciousness. It is said that once we enter this new consciousness, we will see the future history of the whole universe flash before our eyes, yet we will be unable to communicate anything of it to anyone not in the same state of awareness. Perhaps this is why many great mystics have been unable to communicate to ordinary people, choosing instead silence, song, koan, or paradox to explain their experience of the inexpressible.

To master this state, we have to travel through the intense energies of time—meeting, healing, and integrating all the experiences of all our lifetimes. This is a powerful journey that all of us are taking right now, integrating many lifetimes of experience in order to be present at this ending of a huge galactic cycle, and the beginning of another. In this process we learn to live in the present, bringing every part of ourselves back together again, weaving ourselves into the web of life. In doing so, we become conscious co-creators and live our soul's purpose fully, giving freely of our gifts to humanity.

The Galactic Center's infinitely dense point of concentrated mass is a singularity—a totally one-pointed focus. This is the goal of many meditation practices and is known in sacred geometry as the Bindu point, where all aspects of consciousness, all parts of the fragmented mind, body, and soul, all wounds and misperceptions, converge into one single point. As this convergence occurs, we reenter the Great Singularity from which we all came, and a new earth and new form of human being can emerge.

THE INDIAN VIEW

In India, the Sanskrit sound *hal* represents the black hole, the Galactic Center around which all the notes, sounds, and letters of creation are playing. Interestingly, the whole structure and meaning of the Sanskrit alphabet shows this journey through sound. In the *Maheshwara Sutra,* perhaps one of India's preeminent sources on sound, Sanskrit is seen as the alphabet of creation, with each sound forming a different aspect of creation. Together, all the sounds weave a story of a spiraling wave of light moving throughout the creation, forming perception and matter, painting a picture of the harmonious unfolding of vibration and meaning in the various forms of the creative process.

This wave then dissolves back into the formlessness of the Galactic

Center. It leaves the creation it has just created, only to reappear as a wave of eternal light, then to dissolve again, and so on, forever repeating itself in the journey and transformation from form into formlessness into form. This cyclic pulse—particle and wave—is the "beat" of time and space, showing matter and mind as forever appearing and disappearing, faster than our senses can register its movements and forms.

Continual Birthing

Continual birthing is the process of birthing yourself in each and every moment. This birthing allows us to continually recreate ourselves and to birth anew. In letting go of every past moment and embracing the newness of the present moment, we come into the power to create who we are, and what we want to express and share with others.

In the experience of being reborn in every moment, we have the power to choose again who we are, what we feel, what we think, and how we choose to respond to the same situation that is presented to us. We can seize this moment and allow the birthing to take place. This birthing sets in motion a whole stream of new moments, each moment holding infinite possibilities for new creations and new ways of being.

Continual birthing is how we co-create with this infinitely creative wave. We realize, and we choose again and anew as we align to this subtlest, yet most powerful, creative flow as it manifests itself through the dynamism and transparency of living form. It dissolves that which we no longer have need for, that which limits us. It conceals that which you know you have, but which has yet to manifest in your life. It reveals that which accelerates your evolution with the unexpected meeting, person, event, or situation.

Creation flows through us, vibrating our bodyminds at 570 trillion Hz per second. We are moving incredibly fast every single second of our lives—we are just not aware of it. We are birthing and rebirthing every single moment, moving with this wave, this dance happening every single moment. It is the threadlike link between the material and the formless realms, flowing through us and all things perpetually, without ceasing.

Continual birthing in the Galactic Center shows us that this is the Wheel of Life—the hollow bone, the sacred hoop through which life sings us, through which Spirit moves, through which the song is sung via the conduit of our bodies. This is the "everything and nothing," the magic of nothing working within the loving field of everything. And this is within us now.

THE SCIENCE OF
THE GALACTIC CENTER

The Galactic Center is the gravitational center of the Milky Way galaxy. It can also be detected by listening for the "sounds" it creates, sound here being energy carried by gravitational waves. NASA's Chandra X-ray Observatory has detected these sound waves, recording a "note" that is the deepest ever detected from any object in the universe. In musical terms, the pitch of the sound generated by the black hole translates into the note of B flat, 57 octaves lower than middle C, a frequency over a million, billion times beyond the limits of human hearing.

The image from NASA of this black hole also shows two vast bubble-shaped cavities, each about fifty thousand light years wide, extending away from the central supermassive black hole. These two cavities, which are bright sources of radio waves, are not really empty, but are filled with high-energy particles and magnetic fields. They push hot X-ray-emitting gases aside, creating sound waves that sweep across hundreds of thousands of light years. The tremendous amounts of energy carried by these sound waves have already solved longstanding problems in astrophysics by explaining some details of the formation of the universe.

The vacuum of a black hole is made of a perfect circle. If we draw lines radiating out from a perfect circle, they all meet in an optical illusion known as *pragnanz*—a circle that is there but not there, as it is not actually drawn, but formed by the lines themselves.

The lines are infinite emanations of this vacuum; they are the void in motion, directions of light moving after the initial creation of our universe. The central point or Bindu is the point all lines meet and dissolve into. This central point is the goal of many meditation practices, where all thoughts, feelings, and perceptions are concentrated. By entering this point of intense focus, you go beyond it into "no point," or boundless space.

In pragnanz, there is no difference between the lines and the vacuum itself: the lines and the infinite circle are the same. These are described in quantum physics as null lines, the paths taken by light rays and mass particles that have no mass. Indeed, a geometry based on null lines alone is the grail of quantum physics, for in a universe having such a geometry, mass does not exist. All null lines always have zero length, with scale and distance also being zero.

In other words, all distances, times, and notions of large and small, micro and macro no longer exist; therefore no time would elapse during travel from one point to another. In these terms, not even one second passes from the time you leave, say Sirius, to the time you arrive on Earth, for along such a null line the distance to the stars is zero. When you look along a null line, nothing separates you from all that you see in the universe around you. In fact, you are everything that you perceive around you in all directions—there is no separation.

The Web of Life
Intuitive Matrix of Creation

THE WEB OF LIFE IS a pulsing breathing envelope of Shakti that connects all living beings on Earth from animals to humans, plants to trees to stars and beyond. The web networks together all life-forms without discrimination. It works through our etheric bodies, connecting through our auric fields to all other life-forms.

The web and its songlines are how we stay in tune with the environment and each other on an intuitive level, as through the web we can sense what is happening in the flow of life force even many miles away. The ways to tap into this intuitive understanding are well known to animals and indigenous societies worldwide.

The web is different from the Light grids that surround our planet, in that it is the life force that supports the grids, not just on this planet but all planets. The web has always been here, and will never go away. Our connection to it has been disrupted over time, resulting in the current ecological crisis on Earth and separation from feminine wisdom.

We stay connected to the web of life through acts of offering, giving, service, and gratitude. Offering to the web of life all of what you have makes sacred who you are. It feeds the web, and the web in turn feeds you. The web is in a state of perpetual creating, undulating, pulsing. It is as alive as you and me, and infinitely intelligent. In actively supporting life-giving energies or acts of procreation, we can tune in to the web of life and allow it to guide us. In the initial experience of connecting to the web you can literally lose your small self's sense of identity, immersing into this pulse that is behind all life.

The web of life connects all dimensions, and is anchored on Earth in the womb of the world. Webs are nonhierarchical, nonpatriarchal; they are cooperative in nature, which is how they connect us to Earth and beyond. It is this web that has, throughout history, furnished humanity with information that has lead to leaps in our spiritual evolution.

Working with the web of life allows one to be completely present with the energies of the earth, and to thereby gain access to many other dimensions. In the past this connection was done through sound and ritual. It is through this connection that we become aware of our environment and merge with it. And by connecting to it we heal and align ourselves to the natural rhythms and motions of life.

We connect to the web of life by offering, and giving ourselves to it. When we do so, we are taken into the oneness that all life shares. The "I" becomes lost in the one that connects our hearts.

♣ Connecting to the Web of Life

The web can be seen as a glowing silver-white web, threading, weaving, and sustaining harmony in all things. Your body, your flesh, your nerves, your cells, and your very being are permeated by this web.

Offering ourselves sincerely to the web allows us access. Giving something that is important to us directly to the earth—our energy, our desires, our sincere heartfelt prayers and gratitude—rather than just taking (particularly at sacred sites) allows us conscious access. In the offering we receive, and become the conduit, the circuit that is in constant flow, receiving and giving through the open heart of gratitude.

Initially, the best way to do this practice is while visiting a sacred site in nature, where you feel resonance, where you feel at home. Sit down at twilight (or at night if the moon is visible), in a place near some trees and away from city lights, city noise, and interference, if possible.

1. Take off your shoes and sit barefoot on the earth. Focus on your heart. Breathe. Now focus on your feet, and the field of energy that extends down from the feet into the earth. Visualize it.

2. Breathe down through the soles of your feet into this field. Push down the breath, and visualize the field extending.

3. Now extend this field of energy from your feet into Gaia downward; deep down. Allow yourself to plunge down, through the soil, through the many layers of rock, earth, and fire, into the womb of the earth. This is a vast, black, all-enveloping space. Sit here for a moment.

4. Now ask, and pray to Mother Gaia, in your own words, from your own heart, to feel and extend your connection to her. Offer her yourself, offer her your service, and thank her for being your foundation, your anchor, your home. Breathe into this connection, connecting heart, womb, feet, to Gaia. Feel this space within you. For it is part of you, and you are part of it, as part of your origins, your roots, and your foundation.

5. Now open your eyes, and focus on a tree, or a group of trees. Soften your gaze until it becomes slightly blurry. Start to see the aura of the tree, the energy field surrounding it. Be patient. Follow the field of the tree in its expansion outward. See or visualize a silver-white thread or web extending outward and upward, to the moon. Look up to the moon, and feel your feet.

Welcome to the web of life.

In the Native American tradition, Grandmother Spider spins the web of life. From within her belly she spins her web outward, creating the worlds. If we were to feel ourselves as Grandmother Spider, we realize we too can spin webs from our wombs, attracting all we need to us. We do not lack anything, and we have all we need to create and manifest a home, good relationships, and our soul's purpose.

When the time comes to move on from one cycle of time or period of manifestation, like Grandmother Spider we can simply draw all the cords and web connections back into our womb, and move on to another location, to then weave again the web of life and connection.*

We all hold the power to weave ourselves into the web of life, to bring us all we need to be abundant, sustained, and connected. However, for many of you there has been a break, a partial severing stemming from forgetfulness of your connection to the radiant web of life. You have forgotten how to weave this web, as it has been obscured by the wounds and hurts you carry in the womb.

THE WOMB MANDALA

The web of life is spun from your womb—your center of gravity, joy, and creative power. This is your magnetic connection to the web of life. From here, you emanate and draw in energy from the people and environments around you.

There are many wounds and barriers within the womb that inhibit the flow of full power and expression. We leak energy from these wounds, and allow much negative energy to enter that should not be there. These energies can dissipate our potency, empowerment, and creative potential.

The womb opens through right relationship. Having the right discernment and correct boundaries allows the womb to feel safe, nurtured, and free to bloom and express itself. Right relationships are about knowing who your allies are, and who is taking something from you or feeding off your energy in an unhealthy way.

Energies, people, and relationships connect to your womb in ways you may have no idea about. Old lovers, deceased people, people who wish you no good, all of them can be attached to your womb and draining your energy. If we do not know what, and who, is in our wombs, we

---

*Thanks to Star Wolf for this insight about Grandmother Spider and the web of life.

cannot have the appropriate boundaries as to what, and who, should be in our wombs, and what should not be.

One of the quickest ways to identify and clear draining patterns, people, and obstacles from the womb is to place your womb in right relationship through the womb mandala. This mandala works on the four directions that we orient ourselves by in order to live in harmony with the web of life.

To clear out unhealthy relationships, you move them out of your womb. You also place all the relationships that you are engaged in into positions that best allow your womb to flourish. It is a delicate balance, but one that your womb needs to have in order to trust and open.

৪ Womb Mandala Practice*

1. Draw out 3 wide concentric circles. The first circle has a central point. This central point is YOU.
2. Sit silently, and clear your mind. Breathe deeply into your womb.
3. Place your hands on your womb. It is a sphere, a circle. Now visualize yourself in the center of this circle and begin calling in all the people and relationships that your womb is connected to, to make themselves known.

Your Primary Relationships

1. Seeing yourself in this center, look behind you and see who is standing there. Do not allow the mind to dictate, or put who you would like to be there. Just be present, open, and curious, and see with your inner eye who is standing directly behind you. Note that this person could be alive or deceased.
2. Then look in front of you, breathe, and feel who is standing there.
3. Continue this and look to your left. Which person is there?

*This practice was originally published in *The Christ Blueprint: 13 Keys to Christ Consciousness* (Findhorn, Scotland: Findhorn Press, 2009).

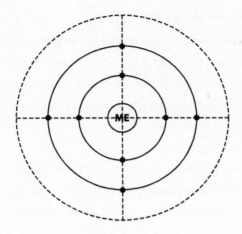

The womb mandala

4. Look to your right. Who is standing there?

These are the primary relationships that your womb is engaged in.

Your Secondary Relationships

Now you are going to create a second circle around this primary circle of relationships. Proceed in exactly the same way.

1. Who is behind the person behind you?
2. Who is in front?
3. Who is to the left?
4. Who is to the right?

This creates a second circle.

Your Most Hidden Relationships

Now proceed exactly in the same way with the third and final circle. This last circle is the periphery. These are the most hidden and seemingly least significant relationships. To create it, simply look around the whole periphery of the second circle and see who is there. Different images and people may float up.

Reading Your Womb Mandala

Your mandala will picture you in the center, surrounded by 3 circles of other beings. You will see 3 beings to your front, 3 behind you, 3 to your left, and 3 to your right. It is often surprising to identify the people who are energetically active in our lives.

In Front = your guides and teachers
Behind = your protectors / supporters / strength
To the Right = male power / soul brother / friend or partner
To the Left = feminine love / soul sister / friend or wife

The first circle of people, those who are closest to you, are those you value the most. They are the most supportive of you, and nurturing toward you, and you are nurturing to them in turn. These people are the ones you allow into your deepest and most intimate space.

The second circle of people are those you connect to through your womb. They have a strong impact on you and are considered to be "close."

The peripheral circle is people that you trust, although they may not be as close to you as the others. All 3 circles represent those people who have the most influence in your life. They are the ones you allow to directly affect you, and who you have let into your womb and the deeper aspects of yourself.

Take a look again at all the beings in your womb mandala. Do you feel a closeness and warmth with all these beings? Is everyone there in full support of your growth? Do any of these beings deplete your energy? Who do you feel is not in his or her right position? What does this mean for you?

For example, if your husband is on your left, in the feminine position, then there is an imbalance in your relationship—he should be on your right. This does not mean that all men should be on your right, but it does make it clear that if you are in intimate relationship with a man, then you are using more of your masculine qualities and he is using more of his feminine ones. If you have a man who is not your partner, but a friend or other loved one, this could indicate that he holds a feminine space for you. Similar wisdom holds true for a man who finds a woman on the right side of his womb mandala.

If there are people in the mandala who you know do not support you, or who you have there out of guilt or obligation, then you have to question this, and maybe move them out to the periphery or completely out altogether. Who is it you want in your womb space? This is not about judging anyone, but about discerning where your boundaries are, and who you let into your womb space.

Clearing Negative Energies from Your Womb Mandala

If you have noticed that there are energies present in your womb mandala that do not serve your highest potential, you have to take action. You can take energetic action by cutting cords or commanding with power that these people leave, or you can simply send them love and wish them goodbye. Alternatively, the situation may require you to take direct physical action. You may have to end a relationship, or spend less time with an individual. You may need to ask someone for forgiveness, or offer it.

Clearing out old energies is simple:

1. Charge up your womb by breath, intention, or by doing the Shakti Circuit.
2. Hold the person, place, or situation in mind.
3. Command three times, or more, for them to leave.

It is your womb, not theirs.

If you feel you have correct relationships, you will feel supported, nurtured, and nurturing in your daily life. You will have a clearer connection to the web of life, and will be more able to manifest your heart's passion and desires in a tangible way.

Keep doing the womb mandala every morning and evening to facilitate this clearing. Keep checking in with yourself. It eventually only takes a minute or two to do, and you become centered in your womb awareness so that you no longer even need to do it; it becomes an automatic feeling and knowing. You get to know what is good for your womb, what nourishes and feeds it, what it wishes to share. You also get to know what it does not need, what does not nourish it, and discern what to allow in, and what not to allow in.

As you clear out your womb you become more aware of what is lurking in there. You might be hanging onto someone deceased, or to old lovers, or to people trying to drain your energy. Or you could be too attached to an experience, person, or environment that is toxic for you. In this exploration, you can become more aware of your connection to the whole web of life. As this connection deepens, more stored memories surface. You may choose to do womb mandalas every week, and in new situations in which you find yourself. Notice the changes that occur.

PART THREE

Shakti Awakened

Shakti and the Source of Love

Aligning with Your Soul's Purpose

EVERY JOURNEY OF SOUL CONSEQUENCE begins at a doorway, face to face with a guardian or a test. Sacred vows and a sincere commitment are needed before you can enter this doorway, and once you make that commitment you must have the bravery to step into the unknown, even though it may be frightening. You will go through the fire, and encounter a deeper, intuitive knowing about the worlds that lies beyond appearances. This bridge into a vaster reality is the world of the daimon.

THE DAIMON

The daimon is your inner friend or guide, your guardian angel. It is found in all traditions, as the Roman *genius,* the Arabic genie or *jinn,* the shaman's spirit helper, or the Christian's guardian angel. In the original theology angels were called *daimons;* the idea of guardian angels came from the Greek notion of a personal daimon.

Daimons are intermediary spirits between human beings and God, acting as spiritual advisors. They are often portrayed either as angelic beings of light or as animal spirits, and they serve as the motivation and inspiration for spiritual force or genius. They manifest as the voice of the soul—as the feelings of unrest that exist in us and force us into the unknown, where we find self-destruction and/or self-discovery.

In this sense daimons are different from what are called angels today; they are powers of transformation that speak to us through dreams, symbols, and dramatic events in our lives. They live between spirit and matter as messengers, inhabiting the place where light and dark meet. They are beyond the duality of good and evil, and use either polarity at any time in order to make you whole. They live in the space between what we today call angels and demons, and they hold the gateway to the rich mine of spiritual wealth known as the "golden shadow"—where our highest potential lies.

The Christian tradition has diluted the power of the daimon to mask the true imagination and creative potential of these spirits within all of us, who not only soothe us, but provoke our egos, breaking our boundaries and the limiting belief systems that subtly control our lives in order to liberate us into our highest potential.

We are assigned a daimon at birth to govern and direct our lives. The daimon acts as a guardian: as the force of fate and an accompanying guide who remembers your soul mission and Calling even when you may forget. The daimon motivates, protects, and persists, resisting compromise and reason, often forcing us to turn our lives upside down when we are off track.

Our daimons are the imaginative blueprints of our lives. They hold the keys to our personal legend, which we are bound to follow for our own highest good. It is the voice that calls us to our true purpose, our vocation. The daimon is your inner partner in a relationship designed to fulfill your soul's purpose. The daimon's face differs for each of us. For those who are lovers, it might take the face of the beloved within. For those who prefer service to the world and family as their main practice, it could appear as the Divine Mother. For those who are on the path of high thought and wisdom, it is the inner mentor. For artists, it is the Muse of inspiration who pushes them to their creative and human limits in order to create beauty.

Your Soul's Purpose

Each of us has a divine mission and purpose in this life that demands our commitment and focus. And that mission is expressed by our daimon. The challenge in following our daimon is that it will urge us, at times, in the direction of our fears as a means of overcoming them in order to fulfill our dreams, and our mission.

The demands of the daimonic force upon you can be unorthodox, as it is not only a guiding energy, but a transformative one. It completes the maturation of your soul through the unification of opposing forces within the self, a key part of the opening and healing of the womb. Its source lies in those realms where the Self roots in natural forces, and it is a naturally occurring human impulse or urge within everyone to affirm and increase the Self.

The daimon's inner urgings can come in the form of a sudden journey, a psychological illness, or any radical or unexpected behavior or event designed to shake you up to what is needed for you to grow, and fulfill your mission on Earth. The daimonic force seeks to overcome the obstacles to development, whatever the cost.

We each have a responsibility to follow our dreams, and not give up on them. In order to uncover our mission, we must abandon many of our conditioned ideas of right and wrong, of what makes "sense" and what does not, and step into the intuitive imagination, or Shakti. Following our soul's purpose, or dreaming of a better life and "going for it" is a requirement of happiness. You might establish a level of contentment without it, but that is not happiness.

When you dream and challenge yourself to overcome your fears and doubts, your life will go through a period of hardship, just as it does when you begin exercising for the first time in years: you feel out of shape and have to go through a period of feeling bad before you can feel good. As you break out of the mold you were stuck in, you will find that individuals will try to sabotage you. They may say that you cannot do what you're intending to do, or that you are crazy. All they are really saying is, "I don't want you to succeed because if you do, I have to look at my own lack of fulfillment." And many people are afraid to do that, so they try and knock you back down to their level, back into the box.

The daimon is the incorrigible Will to fulfill and achieve our humanity through this natural innate force, which we are all born with, but which many lose at puberty. This force has the power to overwhelm and possess you. The daimonic force (unlike the demonic force, which is merely destructive) has no qualms about ideas of good and bad, as it sees both polarities coming from the same source: the power of our highest human potential. Each person's daimon has the "right" answers for that person, regardless of whether that information makes logical sense. It is impossible to trust this divine voice if we make choices based on an outside voice.

At whatever level we live in the spirals of evolution, the next one above serves as our daimon. This is a fundamental law of energy; we cannot solve problems or dissolve obstacles by working at the same level of energy where the problem is. We have to go to the next octave in order to resolve the issue. For those near, or in enlightenment, the daimon or guide is God itself, rather than a Master, showing that our real task in evolution is to obtain God in the daimon's place. Thus daimons are not fixed, but unfold in relation to our own spiritual development, changing face over time as we transform and evolve.

Those who become aware of their daimon will eventually become aware of their true Self, as the daimon is the portal to the One. Your daimon can usually only be accessed when you are at a threshold, the gates of a breakthrough. However, having a daimon does not make you immune to suffering. Instead, it accelerates even the hard lessons in our lives, for the daimon drives us relentlessly toward the one-pointed goal of becoming the center. What our daimon teaches us, therefore, is not to always be seeking a cure for our suffering, but rather to seek a use for it, a channel to direct this force into, so that we may create something out of it.

It manifests as the voice within, and will protect you, but only the "You" who serves its plan for your true Self. It will guide you, and as it is grounded in the impersonal Ground of Being itself, you will inevitably be guided into the One.

EMBRACE AND ALLOWING

Allowance is opening the door to the acceptance of your own divine nature, and also of your basest human nature. In allowance you come to see the truth about yourself, and let the pain, the sadness, the anger, the grief, and the unworthiness bubble up and be in you, simply allowing it to be present. Allowance is the radically honest acknowledgment of what you feel may make you look small or weak, knowing that this sense of humility will enable you to be free, and open to love ever more deeply.

In allowance you open the heart, allowing it to be touched by something far greater than you, and in a felt sense you "give way" to this feeling of love. You melt all that is rigid within more readily and easily, the more you practice it. Allowance is the open expression, the radically honest acknowledgment of what you feel may make you look small or weak, knowing that this sense of humility will enable you to be free and ever more deeply open to love.

And this, my friends, leads to acceptance. Acceptance is the ultimate initiation. It melts and softens all hardness into the truth of what you really are. True acceptance is not accepting things stoically merely to keep the peace; this compromises your power and your dignity, undermining your self-worth when you know something is right but refuse to say it.

True acceptance is an embrace of what you find unacceptable. You enfold what is presented to you, then extend this enfolding out toward the person, idea, or event that gave rise to the situation. Embracing takes whatever you feel is unacceptable, makes it transparent, and then goes one step further: it makes you bring that vibration of the unacceptable inside your heart, and then moves your heart to envelop, embrace and extend itself into that vibration. And this is love, as Mother Mary,

Mother Theresa, and countless other mothers and lovers throughout history have shown.

♣ Conscious Embrace

What can you not stand, what do you find totally unacceptable in the world, in your relationships, and in yourself? What turns you OFF, what repels you, what makes you want to run away? What do you hate? What is the last thing you would do in the world? What is the most unacceptable action, thought, or words that you would ever say, think, or do?

1. Name 7 things that you would not do. Write them down, in detail, and place the paper in front of you. If you have more than 7, write them down also; in fact, write down as many as you can think of.

2. Now, look at the first thing on your list. Evoke the feeling of what this brings up in you. Go into the feeling qualities in the body. Does it evoke anger, resentment, a sense of righteousness or injustice?

3. Just be present with whatever arises. Pay attention to the thoughts that are ignited. Now return to the feeling of it. Observe what is happening within. Perhaps tightness, constriction, pain, tears, sadness—simply let it be. Stay with it and breathe deeply and consciously into your heart. Do this 7 times. No matter what resistance you feel, breathe it deeply into your heart seven times, and hold it there.

4. Now embrace it. No matter how unacceptable, horrific, wrong, cruel, it may seem. Just embrace it. Just allow the feeling to be there, and yet still breathe into the heart and allow the heart to embrace it. What happens within you?

Now repeat this process for the remaining 6, or more, unacceptable things; this should take about 20 minutes if you do it properly. Repeat this practice whenever and wherever these feelings arise—in the car, at dinner, or at home.

Hugging the Unacceptable

Another way to do this practice of conscious embrace is to actually meet the person you find most unacceptable.

1. Go up to this person and hug him or her. While hugging, focus on your heart, and breathe in the quality you find most unacceptable about this person.
2. See this quality as innocent, and a part of you also. Embracing it in another allows you to embrace it completely in yourself. Recognize that this person is, in fact, one of your greatest teachers on love.

Acceptance and embrace bring peace to our lives. No matter what situation we are in, if we accept what it is, without judgment, something new will happen because we have changed our perspective. The control of the mind melts into softness and contentment, and the need to judge and compare also dissolves. Acceptance brings us closer to our own authentic self, so we can see clearly the next step forward without the mind's control.

This all starts with your own self. Be the mother to your own self, love and accept all your weaknesses and failings. Loving yourself for who you are in this moment is the foundation of acceptance. When you accept yourself in this way, you can accept others. You recognize that they, too, are like you; perhaps with different strengths and weaknesses, but just like you, growing, struggling, moving.

"I Love and Accept Myself Exactly as I Am"

Living this attitude means you can handle anything, and anyone, that comes to you. You can identify and provide for them what their soul is asking for behind the pain, the anger, and the projection. You understand that the pain and anger we all feel at different times simply masks a wound, a need for love; a need to give love, receive love, to be loved and loving.

To see this truth, the innocence that lies behind yours and others' anger, means you are able to see with the eyes of love. You see where love is missing, and how to bridge the gap with a total embrace. This is a powerful act of love that goes beyond the personal; it is unconditional love.

RUTHLESS COMPASSION: WIELDING THE SWORD

The sword is the power of discriminating wisdom that separates the beneficial and nonbeneficial actions that must be taken in your life. It is the power of wisdom and will in direct action that cuts away any illusion. The sword is the power to cut away all that is useless, destructive, and resistant to change. It simply says no to anything that is negative, and cuts away the expected roles that you feel you have to live, which only serve to keep you small or limited.

The sword of compassion cuts away all that keeps you locked into the small self and its needs, hopes, and attachments that limit the shining of your light. It cuts away all expectations that you place on yourself, and all expectations you place on others. It cuts in order to reveal something new, a new possibility where once before there was deadwood or old baggage.

This sword vanquishes ignorance, and creates discernment and detachment through the exercise of willpower. By cutting through illusions and leaving behind egoic actions that only lead to more unhappiness, you become clear. You strengthen your soul's power, abilities, and purpose. Your soul grows each time you use the sword correctly because doing so validates an aspect of divine power, love, and wisdom.

The sword is the protector of the sanctity of the soul. It protects and chastises you when you forget what you are here for—your soul's purpose. It transmits fire. The sword conquers and transmutes the darkness and chaos of the mind. It can be frightening as well as purifying. Indeed, statues of Mary in many churches throughout southern France

Mary, nurturer and protector

are commonly depicted holding a sword in the right hand, and a baby in the left.

Owning and using this power of the sword requires ruthless compassion. Anything that stands in the way of your growth must be cut away: any attachment, any fear, any person that distracts you from your goal. This is the ruthless cutting through of any and all illusions, veils, and ignorance to awaken your soul. It is death to the ego and total surrender to Self.

The heart of ruthless compassion is the heart of spaciousness that allows others to be in their pain and suffering so they may grow. It is destructive force harnessed to Divine Will and it has no remorse. It is relentless in that it is not affected by others' suffering; it sees all without hiding. Once started it can never be stopped, until all obstacles and ignorance are destroyed. This is the heart of acceptance, accepting what must be, for the highest good of all.

Ruthless compassion provides rapidly accelerated evolution for those who wish to be fully enlightened, no matter what. In ruthless compassion, one is ready and willing to do absolutely anything to become a channel for Divine Will. This path can appear cruel as it usually involves giving you what you need to grow, rather than what you want; comfort comes last on the list. For this reason, ruthless compassion is often not appreciated until well after it has been received, and can be greeted initially by the ego and shadow with resentment and anger. Imagine your partner being crucified, dying in front of you, while you held his baby in your womb: is this is not the height of ruthless compassion?

Love without power dissolves into a weak, astral fairytale. Love without strength and depth crumbles into an ungrounded, chaotic mess, just as power without love becomes a game of fear and tyranny. Discipline without joy becomes an intense, self-defeating, oppressive hell. In order to flow with ruthless compassion and implement its actions and directions, you must act with great surrender and wisdom. Wisdom here is the ability to see beyond the appearance, to the true clinging, suffering need of a person or situation. Wise action arises from being objective, clear, and direct in understanding how and why the ego protects and cloaks itself at all costs.

Ruthless compassion is not an emotion or feeling. It is a way of being that arises when we are fully dedicated and surrendered to our larger Self, and by extension to all others. It is uncompromising, direct, and unflinching. Ruthless compassion becomes a process of relentless surrender that grinds down anything that stands in the way between your larger Self, and your smaller self.

It witnesses what is happening in silence, and with total Presence. This leads to total harmlessness, as no reaction, no harm can affect you when you have no harm, no violence, no triggers left within you. Then these forces can be wielded in order to serve love most effectively, as and when required.

Directness

Sometimes the bludgeon is required. The bludgeon that cuts to the bone, that illumines illusion in the most direct and uncompromising manner. My friends, do not compromise with the seeing of illusion in yourself and others. Be radically honest, for this serves love. Be brutally frank, be directly engaging, and do not shirk your responsibility toward the growth of the soul. This is true friendship that loves the soul beyond the machinations of the ego and its hopes, fears, needs, and holes.

The sword leads people into, and through, the dark night of the soul, or should I say the dark night of the ego. It builds people's character, strength, power, and light and dissolves their small self, to lead them into joy and loving service, service that will have true impact as it is based on authentic, deep, lived experience of the darkest places that a human being can go into. Once you have lived through this experience of the sword then anything is possible for you, as you have reclaimed your power from the darkness, and can now wield it. Darkness forges the soul into a diamond by burning the dross away, leaving only that which is immortal. Heaven is reached by going through the hell of your own shadow.

Here there is no "your truth" or "my truth"; there is one truth to which we both align. The sword is not here to help you or your illusions, for in the dark night you come to realize that there is no self to help, just the one Self that needs no help, just resting within, and embracing.

THE PYRAMID OF THE MIND

To access our power fully requires that we use the mind to liberate the mind. Mind uses breath and life force as an energy source and distributor of the four elements, and together mind and life force create the circuitry that interconnects every point of the subtle form. With imbalances in the life force, imbalances in mind occur. When balance of life flow occurs, the mind can perform its functions without interfering or taking over the role of the soul. Both work together in order to release and embody more Shakti.

In the science of Indian meditation, the pyramid of mind is built upon the following:

1. The separate mind
2. The judging/discerning mind of the individual will
3. The mind as interpreter between the physical and mental worlds

Together, this trinity of the mind creates our individual identities, giving us the neurological foundation to be separate, unique, and different from others. These energies of mind allow us to say yes and no, to make choices, to have a free will. Our power of choice is created and actualized here, manifested by the vital streams of life flow that power our bodyminds.

The parts of the brain associated with the first level of the pyramid are the parietal lobes and the frontal lobes. The parietal lobes house the Orientation Association Area, or OAA. The function of the OAA is to give us orientation in space. You may take it for granted that you can tie a shoelace or walk through a door, but this is only possible due to intense neurological activity in the rear of the parietal lobes. Scientific research has shown that brain damage to this area makes the smallest tasks, such as grasping a glass of water, impossible, because the injured brain cannot perceive a distinction between the hand, the glass, and the space in between.

On the physical level, the ability to perceive boundaries and distinction is essential for us to carry out tasks. However, our facility to perceive these boundaries also creates in us a sense of separation and aloneness. In the human brain the OAA is chronically overactive. This stimulates the amygdala-hippocampus connection, which connects a pair of brain centers designed to give a sense of meaning to perceptions and events registered as important. If the OAA, which is designed to create a perception of distinction and separation to a useful degree, is hyperactive, we automatically interpret this hyperactivity as evidence that separation is the reality.

With a hyperactive parietal lobe, we become fundamentally and existentially separate from everything we perceive, be it hand, glass, person, Earth, or universe. Everything that we perceive is seen as distinct from us, and we are separate from each object. The sense of small self is created by this function, which the brain creates constantly in reaction to its environments and its need to physically survive.

Neuroscience has shown that in deep meditation or prayer, the OAA in the parietal lobe is temporarily blocked from neurological input. This leads to temporary states of vastly expanded consciousness, as the sense of separate self cannot find its usual boundaries, and expands in order to find them.

The frontal lobes of the brain are associated with individual will. Many mystical traditions speak about the merging of the individual will with the Divine Will, as the doorway to awakening. This cannot happen if the frontal lobes are underactive.

On a subjective level, the signs of underactive frontal lobes are dullness, lethargy, weakened self will, a sheep or follower mentality, loss of ability or curiosity to question, submissiveness, and boredom. This just about sums up the state of much of humanity for the last few thousand years—easily manipulated, first by religious authorities, and now by the media, advertising, governments, peer pressure, and so forth.

Chemically, dopamine is the essential neurotransmitter for frontal lobe activity; it is also necessary for feelings of bliss. Lack of dopamine increases a person's urge to control and maintain his or her small self will, not letting the mind expand beyond a certain threshold. It is like dying—a person whose life was full, their purpose lived out and completed, can let go and have a more graceful death than a person who feels something is missing in his or her life. The unfulfilled person will cling more to life.

When the frontal lobes are activated, a full flowering of the individual will into the greater will can occur; there is no more separation. Without full activation of the frontal lobes and dopamine saturation, the trinity of the mind cannot find its rightful place as servant of the soul. And this is why the trinity of mind has been created—to anchor your will into Divine Will, so you may become an agent of your soul's purpose, which leads to your deepest fulfillment and highest potential.

When the frontal lobes are fully activated (*buddhi* in Sanskrit), it is the highest form of mental function we have. This aspect of mind is responsible for the underlying decisions, choices, and actions we make in everyday life. It knows when to engage or when to abstain from action, and the right time to do or say something, as well as the right time to NOT say or do anything.

It is fluid intelligence as opposed to rigid intellect—the application of wisdom in any situation as opposed to just knowledge or rote understanding/dogma. Buddhi understands which actions lead to more love and freedom, and which actions do not, as the root meaning of *buddhi* is "to awaken," or more specifically, "a bridge to awakening."*

Identification with this sense of individuality leads to judgment, and the twinned forces of desire and aversion, push and pull, attraction and fear, bliss and terror, which culminate in the fear of death. These qualities make up the second point of the pyramid of mind. Judgment and the tendency to compare one thing or person to another are the distortions of this aspect of mind; discernment is its true function.

Discernment is the ability to see the whole picture of a situation without a charge, from the heart and mind united. In this seeing, we witness what is occurring from a neutral place, without getting involved

---

*Paradoxically, it is also through the buddhi that the notions of a separate soul become manifest, for time is a concept marked and measured by the buddhic mind, a mind that is connected to the natural rhythm of life, which intuitively links into universal rhythms of timing and flow.

in giving it a value. This allows the witness in your heart to discern an appropriate response, (or not) which will be unique for each soul at any moment.

The difference between judgment and discernment is the assignment of value—the value of being right or wrong, good or bad. Judgment divides and labels—and attaches value—whereas discernment weighs a situation based on a unified heart-mind connection. If you have an emotional charge or wound, then judgment occurs.

The ego, or *manas,* is the third aspect of the mind, acting as the interpreter between the physical and mental worlds. The manas is the link between these two worlds, mediating and holding the tension between them. All the energies of the life flow function only when connected by ego. If the mind is not connected to life flow, the senses cannot make any sense of what is happening to it, or around it, for it is only through mental contact that one can understand objects. The body needs the mind to survive—without body there is no mind, without mind there is no body. If one dies, the other dies.

The manas runs and maintains this mental-physical feedback loop. When this aspect is overactive it generates the experience of limitation because the mental and physical worlds becomes the only reality, and anything outside of this reality, outside of the mind and senses, gets labeled as impossible or ridiculous. Only the perception of the intellect and of physical matter are registered as real.

The reliance on this aspect of the mind is what dominates society today, generating cynicism, short-term planning, rigidity, adherence to dogma, and aversion to anything out of the box. And, of course, this aspect of mind also leads into the consensus reality model, where because the masses or authorities agree on something, that is how it is.

The three functions of the automatic mind all interconnect and overlap in form and function. They are designed to serve our souls like a servant, allowing the soul to flow freely and with maximum efficiency, to express and create joy and share love. When these three are working in harness with the soul and witness consciousness, a balanced and heart-centered society can manifest.

The mind has been created to help us function and evolve optimally. The problem is that for most of the world the soul is currently enslaved to these three aspects of the mind. Instead of the soul running the mind, the mind is running the soul. Imbalance reigns. By constantly giving voice to and going along with this reversal, you continue its survival as master. By expressing the false, you give it more hold and energy and manifest it into this reality. What you think and say, you become.

THE WITNESS

In self-inquiry you learn to witness your thoughts, and you begin to see everything differently. When we witness, the mind becomes a movie to watch. Think of your life as a TV movie—witness the vast numbers of different channels, programs, and vibrations, just like the thoughts and events in your life. Watch all the events you have participated in, all the different actors, all somehow connected to the same underlying script. Can you see yourself?

When we accept both sides of a perspective, not fighting or struggling, then we can automatically enter into the witness consciousness—the third point. This is invaluable because we cannot solve a problem by working at level where the problem exists—we have to rise beyond it. In his book *I Am That,* the Indian sage Nisargadatta Maharaj explains it this way, "True Awareness is a state of pure witnessing without the least attempt to do anything about the event witnessed. Your thoughts and feelings, words and actions may also be a part of the event—but you understand precisely what is going on because it does not affect you."*

The nature of the mind is that it goes on and on and on automatically; all sorts of thoughts arise and keep coming. This continuous activity distorts every experience you have, consuming a lot of energy.

---

*Nisargadatta Maharaj, *I Am That: Talks with Sri Nisargadatta Maharaj* (Durham, N.C.: Acorn Press, 1990).

For the witness mind, the mind works when it is needed; and when it is not needed it just stops. It stops when you realize you are not in control, that there is nothing that you can do about it.

You may bemoan that thoughts cause so much trouble, but it is the resistance to the thought that causes discomfort or irritation. The problem is not the thought or the mind but the effort expended, the aversion, to change the thought. You need not push or pull something to or from yourself, or struggle. In neither pushing away the ugly nor holding on to the beautiful, your identification with the thoughts, and the feeling that you create these thoughts, will be gone.

One Mind

There is not your mind, or my mind. There is only ONE mind of the collective consciousness. The nature of the mind has never changed—this is what makes it the mind. There is no point in wanting to change this structure of the mind, as much as you cannot change the nature of a tiger, or the nature of fire. You cannot say your oxygen is mine, for we are all breathing the same atmosphere. Similarly you are breathing this mind. You cannot get rid of this mind. You can only be free of it by realizing that it is not yours; then you will stop trying to change it.

This ancient mind is what has characterized humanity since the time of the Neanderthal, for this ancient single mind is based on fear. Earlier it could have been the fear of a tiger or lion; today it is fear of relationship, of being vulnerable, of change, of losing your job. The same craving is there; the same desires are there, only the appearance of the objects of craving, fear, anxiety, have changed. But the desire to be or have something else is still there.

This mind will never stop trying to reach somewhere, never stop trying to achieve something. Rarely does the mind pose questions to get answers, but simply to stay alive—it is its survival mechanism. Keep watching this mind, which always has doubts, fears, and questions to ask, and will always try to understand. This is the mechanism of the mind. It will never lead to the "peace that surpasses all understanding." Mind and "you" are nothing but a bundle of questions.

All these questions, cravings, to arrive somewhere, to be somebody . . . are not yours! They are the one collective ancient mind of humanity. All thoughts, all sufferings are of the total human race. One mind only is there for everybody. This is why the Bodhisattva Vow is so appropriate—only when everybody is free from suffering will suffering truly end, and until then the Bodhisattva works to liberate all beings.

When we witness the one ancient mind, we can leave it behind. This transformation does not focus on a transformation within the mind, as psychologists and philosophers do; this is becoming free of the mind itself.*

Once you are in the Witness you find that you love what you see, whatever may be its nature. This choiceless love is the touchstone of Awareness. If this love is not there you are not in the Witness.†

The Witness Consciousness sees that there are only personalities arising in space and disappearing. Who you think you are is nothing but a set of discontinuous personalities, arising and disappearing so quickly that you cannot see it under normal circumstances. These personalities arise and cease in an ever-continuing process. Ultimately, whether the self feels big or small, the effort to end the self IS another personality. Watch this also. For you are the vast spaciousness in which all these ideas and personalities appear, and then disappear.

Some may say that self-inquiry and witnessing are more masculine, mental activities, not womb-like or connected to Shakti. However, witnessing and self-inquiry are processes that actually release more Shakti, more energy, by clearing us of beliefs and negative thought patterns. These processes are neither male nor female, and are vital in order for us to reach a non-dual state of being beyond male and female. To be

---

*From a dialogue between Kiara Windrider and Sri Kalki, India, 2005.
†Sri Nisaragadatta Maharaj, *I Am That*.

divinely feminine, you also have to be divinely masculine and hold these qualities within yourself, just as many luminous women, past and present, have shown us.

SELF-INQUIRY

Fortunately, there are tools for helping each of us break free of the habits of mind discussed above. One of these tools is self-inquiry, which is a process of constantly questioning and reversing the tendency to look outside of your true self, looking to your stories and identifications, for the origin of your awareness.

Do you believe everything that your mind tells you?
Have you noticed if you feel irritated when thinking about or feeling the presence of certain people or things?
What if all that is occurring in your life right now is due to the thoughts you are experiencing? Thoughts that are not even yours . . .

Inquiry only arises through curiosity, through being open to learning more in every moment. Examining yourself thoroughly can change the way you feel about yourself, as the unchallenged habits, conditionings, and actions all come under the searching spotlight of your consciousness. Holding yourself gently as you question behaviors that prevent you from empowerment and love is the key to transformation.

Thoughts consist of two aspects. The first is subjective—"I," me or mine. The second is objective—a role or object with which the "I" is involved. The habit of the mind is to get caught in the object, looking outside, and not to look within to recognize the true self.

What we call our "self" is a collection of "I am this" or "this is mine," in which your true self becomes obscured with a fleeting role or object. Self-inquiry consists of discarding the object in order to discover the pure subject. This requires withdrawing our attention from the objects of sensation, emotion, and thought by discriminating and separating these from the self or seer that observes them.

Self-inquiry means holding to the search for the true self in all that one does with one's entire energy and attention, so we do not preoccupy our minds with too much outside stimulation. First, you must discriminate yourself, the seer, from the external objects in your environment. Then you can discover that part of you is a constant Presence, while other parts of you come and go. You learn to discriminate that this part of you, known as the seer, is constant and not altered by fluctuations.

Then, you can discriminate between the seer and emotional or mental states. Thoughts and feelings continually change but the seer, if we look deeply, remains the same. For example, the seer of anger does not cease to be when anger itself passes away. There is a Presence underlying the anger, that once we become subtle enough, we can notice, even if we do not always act upon it immediately!

Here we begin to discriminate between what is present, and what stops us from being present: what is the story, the past, the identity and attachment to who we once were, or thought we were, and no longer are in the present moment. We begin to notice that what drives our actions is a continual strategy of defense, caused by a reaction to the belief that we are separate from a deep, loving resonance of divine Presence. This means that we are not free to live and create in the true sense, and instead act from the mind's desire to avoid the pain and grief that arise from the belief of lack of love, and unmet needs and wants.

Deep self-introspection and inquiry, questioning your beliefs, thoughts, feelings, and assumptions about yourself can work faster with a reference point for truth, a benchmark, a guide of some kind, along with your own inner voice and its promptings. By aligning to Christ Mind, Buddha Mind, or the eighteen pathways whenever thoughts arise, we can challenge the hold that the mind has by gradually replacing these thoughts with those that we know in our heart and soul to be true.

Of course this gradual replacing comes with investigation into what lies behind the thought or feeling. What lies behind the thought or feeling? What is the next layer? And what is the next layer after that? And after that? Keep going until you have unpeeled all the layers of the onion, and you reach the core of the issue. What you may think a problem is can radically change after this investigation.

Question the mind's assumptions; communicate with the mind and create a dialogue between mind and soul so mind can be gently retrained to follow the soul's directives. Self-inquiry is a continuing process and journey. The eternal question "Who am I?" is the first act of self-inquiry. All other inquiries are born from this. The process is continual just as creation is continual, perpetually revealing and unfolding nuances, depths, deeper meanings, and insights. It can be quite fun!

♣ A Self-inquiry Practice

One form of self-inquiry gently asks questions that we drop into our minds and contemplate over the day, without immediately having to provide an answer. Instead, we allow the answer to bubble up naturally, spontaneously, and organically from the soul when it has the answer.

This form of question is best asked as you wake up in the morning, and it can then be allowed to sink into the subconscious mind as you go about your day. The answer may come through a meeting, a conversation, in a meditation, after making love, when going on a walk . . . whenever the conscious mind is relaxed enough to allow a different perspective from your normal one to arise.

So . . . feel into this for a moment. What deep questions do you have about your life that cannot be answered in a minute?

1. As you are waking, when you are still in that dreamy state between sleep and waking, remember one of these questions and ask it.
2. After you have asked the question, give it to the Divine, the voice of your soul; then let it go.

What happens during the day? Does something cause the answer to bubble up spontaneously?

Another form of self-inquiry process arises when we are confused or emotionally overwhelmed.

Here we simply take a few breaths and ask ourselves the following questions:

Can and does this thought, this feeling, this action, lead to more love?

Can and does this thought, this feeling, this action, lead to empowerment?

Can and does this thought, this feeling, this action, lead to more wisdom?

Can and does this thought, this feeling, this action, help others?

If you are honest, humble, and sincerely wish to grow, the answer should become clear. What takes courage is to follow through on the information you have received, even if it means you have to back down from your position, forgive yourself or another, or sometimes look like a fool. You will only look like a fool in the eyes of the ego; in the eyes of the soul you will be a hero, and angels will applaud you for your heroism and love. Most importantly, you will be free to go on to the next stage of your life.

The All-Seeing Eye

The Circuit Completes

IN CONSCIOUS PRESENCE WITH THE flow of Shakti, you complete a Shakti Circuit by moving through each of the eighteen pathways in any sequence that feels right to you. One example of a circuit is described below.

Feel the flow of Shakti from the Alta Major down the spine, fanning through the kidneys to the base of the spine, pulsing through the anus and the perineum, Shakti arrives at the first gate, the lips of the yoni. Sparking through the second and third gates, the Gratitude-spot and the red rose of the clitoris, Shakti arrives at the fourth gate, the diamond of the cervix. Crossing this threshold with sacred intention, Shakti expands into the dark vastness of the womb with each breath. Moving through the fifth gate into the marriage of the masculine and feminine within, you open to receive the jewels of your soul's mission at the sixth gate, and then on through to the doorway of the eternal divine flow.

Having ignited and fired the spirals of creation within the vastness of your being, this flow proceeds from the womb in golden spiraling infinity loops to the heart.* In the connecting from the vastness and

---

*In men, this loop goes from the testicles to the heart. A man's testicles become encased in a golden loop which then rises upward in another, smaller infinity loop to his heart, and back down again, connecting his sexuality to his heart.

power of the womb to the purity of love in the heart, we bridge two separate experiences into one. One cannot create just from heart or womb; both have to be connected and flowing for true empowerment, wisdom, and love to emerge, in balance and universal harmony.

This looping between womb and heart is a natural step in the alchemy of creation. It is within the depths of the heart that you find the purity of the surrender to—and union with—Divine Will. As this golden looping of alchemical flow continues, Shakti begins to flow into the third eye, bringing you to the command center for manifestation into form: the union of the third eye and the mouth of the Goddess (Alta Major) that reveals the all-seeing eye. (M.R.)

SHAKTI
AND THE WITNESS

The power to witness allows us to retract from conflicting situations, to see our own lessons, and not to project or get caught up in any power games with another. All conflicts have their root in our own perception, our own inner conflict. All you need to do is see why you are creating conflict, withdraw from the situation, and own that part of yourself. Witnessing is the key to this.

Witnessing allows you to step out of the way and let Shakti speak through you. As you witness your own self, you train your mind to become a tool rather than the guide. This allows Shakti to use you as a tool, speaking and guiding through the instrument of your body and mind. This flow brings energy and wisdom that you have no idea you possess until the very moment when it comes out of your mouth!

This is an amazing experience to engage with; you are speaking and learning at the same time, and the conscious mind is still. Indeed, the conscious mind can experience amazement, awe, and gratitude as this happens, once it allows Shakti to pulse through. This then

212 ～ *Shakti Awakened*

becomes a normal way of being, as any good teacher or guide will tell you. This is our natural state.

In this state, you have no idea what you are speaking about, or how this speech is happening. It just IS. You access wisdom and the power of transmission directly. This is not channeling. The truth of anything lies within you, and can be accessed at any moment if you can let go of the agendas of your small self with its concepts, boxes, and definitions. This allows the greater Shakti to arise and guide.

When this happens, and as Shakti arises, you are so situated in the present moment that you cannot even remember what you were saying, or how, as it pours out of you. This is how the greatest teachers, artists, and speakers create and reveal the greatest truths and beauty—in the moment, with no idea of what to conceptualize or create. This allows the highest potential for that person or group to manifest.

There is no need to plan once you are in the flow of Shakti. All you have to do is let go, witness the doubting mind—constantly planning and in fear of being in the present, where Shakti lives—and allow. This takes trust, confidence, and the Witness. Of course, the mind has to be prepared, has to be crystallized, to be able to feel safe and secure in letting go into something far greater than itself. For example, if you are giving a complex PowerPoint presentation to corporate clients, you may have to prepare something beforehand. Yet, if during the presentation you can let go, more Shakti can arise, and your clients will feel more of what you are sharing with them, receiving it in a deeper way.

It is our natural state to be in this flow of the moment, where Shakti lives, expresses, and creates. It is not miraculous or extraordinary; it is something we can all do with the Shakti Circuit flowing, active, and alive with the witness to guide and channel the energy. As the witness allows the guiding of Shakti into deeper states of peace and joy, Shakti fulfills its purpose: to reverse the hegemony of the mind so we can live in the flow of life, and in our hearts.

THE BLACK LIGHT OF
THE UNIVERSAL WOMB

The Black Light is the light of the universal womb, before light is visible, before color, before matter, as you know it. This Black Light is the body of Isis; it is what she is clothed in. The universe is pervaded by this tender, loving, presence, holding you, unfolding all that you are, containing all that you are, in the womb.

Before there was light, and an idea of darkness, lies Black Light, the sweet silence of the Beloved calling you home. It is sweet emptiness, the heart surrendered. It feels like your heart is gently, but perpetually breaking wide open. Black light is crystal clarity, pure, deeply touching. There is no object for its love and compassion, no reference point, no concept or form, nothing to hold onto, no memory, no past, no future.

It is the deepest intimacy one can ever know. It embraces you, not you it. It touches you in places nothing else can, and nobody else ever will. It makes you cry, for it is the deepest remembrance of love a human can ever have. It is the beloved that has no face, no form, and no substance. It contains itself completely within itself, pure before it becomes form.

It is only by means of your passage through matter that you evolve. While you are in the stage of your evolution subject to the push and pull of the bodymind or matter, all your sorrows and troubles come to you through your contact with matter. But as soon as you lose your identification with the bodymind, then the Divine Mother can fully manifest.

This Black Light is the dark night of reason. Scientists say that 94 percent of this universe is dark light, a light reachable only beyond the senses. Within this 94 percent lies what we call subspace. This subspace is actually a liquid space, and is felt as a visceral fluid motion, similar to the cerebro-spinal fluid in the center of the spine, which bathes the brain. All obstructions in this pathway must be dissolved to allow the flow of light all the way from the spinal base to the brain. Additionally for women, the womb must also be healed, for the great sufferings of humanity lie within the womb of all women.

Within the womb lies the power of the sun, and within the centers of all suns themselves lies the seed of the Black Light. Suns are grown from the Black Light, and when they explode into supernovas they return into Black Light. The Black Light is the beginning, and end, of creation. When you are born, you come from Black Light in your mother's womb. When you die, you go through the Black Light as your soul makes its journey back to Source.

Creating

The Black Light is the power to create from the space where all things are held in potential before they manifest. Black light is the greatest alchemy, and the most powerful magic of love, the potential that all women hold within the womb. It transforms by holding, and bringing everything that you are back into its pure, undifferentiated, unformed state; original innocence. In this state, all wounds can dissolve, and all things are made possible. All things are made new.

When you create anything of great impact or huge significance that truly taps into universal forces and power, then you to have to enter the Black Light to birth this. Black light, as epitomized in the form of the Black Madonna, is the state from which all realities arise. Christ, Buddha, and other Great Ones, have all had to enter this Black Light to bring forth their transformative actions on the Earth plane, and to ground these actions onto the Earth plane from the radiant light of pure consciousness. As groups, more and more humans can now enact the same type of transformative action, as this power is not limited to individuals anymore.

The quality of the Black Light is the power to birth realities. Every birth, the first and most momentous journey, begins in darkness. Just because humanity has forgotten about it for the last cycle, does not mean that it is not here. It is the height of all alchemy, the heart of transfiguration.

One of the keys to this alchemy is the sacrament of Sacred Marriage, which can lead to direct immersion in the Black Light. It is in this state of being that you both recognize each other as love, as divinely human and as humanly divine, in every cell, in every fiber, nook, and cranny of your bodymind and soul, in every behavior. You include it all. It is here that you Remember and join beings such as Yeshua and Magdalene, among others, who have merged together in the Black Light before, and are still there in that space waiting for you.

Other ways to immerse completely in the Black Light are taught to Egyptian and Tibetan Initiates. In Egypt, these teachings were given to those who had completed the first part of the King's Chamber Initiations, and were ready for the next step. In Tibet these initiations are achieved through mantras to various Dakinis or female Buddhas who have conquered the fear of death.

Darkness

A simple way for you to begin to open to the possibility of Black Light is to spend more time in darkness. Sit in a darkened room in silence, or spend a day and night alone in darkness. Become used to its presence as a living, palpable force. In this darkness make it a practice to embrace the parts of you that arise in fear, restlessness, or judgment. Allow the heart to open and feel in a new way. Make the Black Light your friend. This is a powerful way to enter into it, and get to know yourself better.

To enter into the Black Light, to make it your friend, go back to the beginning of creation. In the beginning there was only darkness, the living waters, and the flow of these living waters when the Creator moved his Light across them. This beginning of creation still lies in all of you today, existing in your bodies in darkness and flow.

Black light is the creative darkness from which all life emerges. We die into darkness so we can experience birth and resurrection, so regeneration can happen. In accessing this darkness, and working within its silence, we guide life from emptiness into form. In the darkness there is so much love that nothing gets in the way of it, nothing reflects it, or refracts it. It is pure, because nothing is there to block it, not even you; not even you are there to limit it. Within darkness there is no duality, nothing to reflect light. Black light is here to birth the infinite possibilities of this space into form.

Many people today are enamored with light, and forget about the darkness, the space from which all light comes, and indeed the place where you are born and nurtured during the first nine months of your life; in the womb. What you give form to in daylight is only 1 percent of what is seen in darkness. If you can access both of these realities, then you can be reborn, if you enter into the process with courage, and embrace all the visions and fears that arise.

John the Beloved, Apostle of Christ, demonstrated his union with the Black Light through his surrender to it. As John intuited the time of his upcoming death, he ordered his disciples to dig a deep hole on top of a hill overlooking Patmos harbor, the idyllic Greek island where he was marooned.

Mystified, they did so, and John asked them to accompany him as he lowered himself into the hole, whereupon he informed them that this was his last night on Earth, and they were to watch over him until the morning. Startled by his request, they stayed up late into the night, listening to their teacher's last words to them. However, in the early hours of the morning, they feel asleep one by one, to wake up at daybreak astonished. John's body was gone, snatched from the embrace of the earth itself. All that was left was an empty, black hole.

Healing

For many of you darkness brings up images of the unknown, what you fear, what you have not yet embraced, what you sweep under the carpet and try to forget about. These locked doors of the human psyche that you fear to step through hold the greatest potential for healing, growth, empowerment, and confidence, for when you fully enter and embrace the darkness, boundaries and limitations expand, dissolving anxieties and fears.

Darkness holds a great deal of power, and empowerment, for you. Complete immersion into darkness through being buried in the earth as part of a shamanic initiation is one of the more powerful portals into the Black Light. In this process of being embraced by the earth, you can heal birth traumas, sexual abuse, and deep wounds through visionary experience, visitation, and richly mythological occurrences, *without* need for modern day methods.

Children hearken back to this kind of initiation by burying each other in the sand. Doing this is one step toward entering a more expanded, healing, magical, and numinous world, where you can speak to spirits past and present, communicate with your ancestors, and enter into multiple realities simultaneously.

When many of you are in darkness together, you all become closer. Many things are revealed about you in the darkness of the Black Light, especially when others are present. All your conditionings and modes of behavior melt and dissolve in darkness, which is when a whole new world of deeper relationship, peace, and wordless feelings communicate your hidden nature.

Here it could be said that light divides, and darkness unites. When whole groups connect and communicate in this way, a family develops. As Christ said, "When more than two are gathered in my name, so there shall I Be." If more than two gather in darkness and silence with the same intention, and commune with each other, a deeper understanding forms, as seen in the rituals of the indigenous peoples of Earth. Sexual impulses and differences can become androgynous and unified as you reconcile your differences back into the night of creation.

This communion is also seen in moments of disaster and huge suffering, when disparate peoples band together in order to help others, sharing everything they have. When this happens on a collective scale, the world will be plunged into Black Light in order to heal as a collective, and to birth a new Earth. This will be a traumatic time for many millions of people, whose deepest, darkest wounds and urges will emerge, as seen in recent disasters when apparently normal people have descended into anarchic states of violence and despair when crisis hit.

This time will be a great purging and transforming. Thousands of evolved beings will balance this suffering through their bodies of light, creating stability for the planetary lightbody. If you feel as though you are one of these people, then get used to the darkness, for it will become your greatest friend in the times ahead.

Embodiment

Living at Your Highest Potential

EMBODIMENT IS THE PRIMARY REASON for the Shakti Circuit. Embodiment means bringing all of your soul into the present, into your body, onto Earth, now. This is how Earth will transform, and how a new civilization will be created. Embodiment is the most rewarding act a human can make, as it involves you becoming the most loving, powerful, and wise person you could ever be. To embody is to live at your highest potential.

The Shakti Circuit is not a transcendent teaching, a way to escape being here now. It is an experiential living in the present designed to bring every part of you back together again, to weave yourself into the fabric of life. Becoming a conscious co-creator by living your soul purposefully, and by giving your gifts to humanity.

The Shakti Circuit uses the keys and primary elements of the creative power in order to bring you into the flow of life. Shakti is the glue that brings all parts of you together. These keys use light, sound, breath, sexual energy, and sacred geometry to reconnect you. In addition, the power of living nature is harnessed and worked with in order to reconnect you to her flow, as a vital part of yourself. Gaia is the anchor point for reconnecting to the Galactic Center. This reconnection aligns with the simultaneous direct reclaiming of power from the shadow, allied with deep inquiry to excavate and release belief systems and old paradigm patterns that block the flow of Shakti.

Breath is the bridge between spirit and matter, the flow of life force. Breathing is the bridge by which light comes into form, illuminating and healing all that it comes into contact with. The more we breathe deeply into Shakti, the more we bring new life into ourselves, releasing the old cellular memories, patterns, and heaviness. It is through the spiral of breath that we reconnect to our DNA, releasing all the latent energy, potential, and universal wisdom held within each and every one of us.

Sexual energy is how all matter is created, how we are birthed into this world, how we are created. It is the juice and fuel for life and creativity itself. In this passion we connect with life, uniting our masculine and feminine into form. It is the current of embodiment, and foundation of manifestation when united with love, power, and soul purpose.

Sacred geometry is the infrastructure for light to manifest itself into the dynamism of living form. It reveals the universal patterns of harmony and balance. When all your geometric structures are activated and in harmony within your heart and mind, they act as a bridge between light and matter, uniting them through the crystalline matrices shared by your DNA, your lightbodies, and your physical body.

Nature as a living being is how Shakti flows through us, showing us how to become embodied. Nature holds the resonance of ourselves, and shows us the laws of creation if we can stop and take a moment to appreciate life. Life force or Shakti weaves us all together. The more we connect to our own life force, the more we connect to nature; the more we connect to the life force in nature, the more we connect to the life force within ourselves.

Inquiry reveals some of your deepest wounds and secrets that harbor your deepest guilt and shame, emotions that prevent you from being open and having a clear heart. By questioning what leads to our life force being blocked, we can release more Shakti. As inquiry deepens into witnessing, we start to observe all that is not aligned to love, wisdom, and power. We start to realize our essential nature by using the mind to go beyond the mind. By training the mind to become a servant of the soul, we attain that which the mind can never fully comprehend, the peace that passes all understanding.

Embodiment entails the descent or ignition of your lightbodies into physical form. Each of these lightbodies has a specific function, and the more we embody each one, the more light we hold in our physical bodies. This also means that you develop more spiritual abilities, and have deeper intuition and communion with all life. As all parts of your soul recongregate and coalesce into your body and conscious awareness, you realize your unity with all life because all parts of you are now woven back together again, in one living tapestry.

THE MUSIC OF THE DANCE

Those who dance not, know not what comes to pass.
CHRIST, IN THE DEAD SEA SCROLLS

Dance enflames and enlivens the soul. It shakes and stretches, it moves and grinds, it celebrates and shifts energies that once activated, can then flow and release. It is prayer in motion, prayer that grooves us into the life rhythm, the organic joy that brings us into the here and now, into our body temples, into relating. It releases and transmutes that which we have held for so long, that which we have repressed, the tears we have not yet shed, the aches and pains, the shock and the grief. A shimmy of the hips and the movement of Shakti through us can transmute all we have suffered into forgiveness.

Dance is our soul's expression of the divine flow; it can be silly, it can be sensual; it can be releasing, it can be joyful; it can be shared or it can be solo; it can be cathartic or it can be exultant. It can express and release any chakra, any emotion; we can feel into, and literally become any chakra or emotion through dance.

Shamanic dance takes us through many layers of our being. Dancing through the layers—through the tiredness, through the pain, beyond your barriers, what you previously knew or felt to be possible or impossible—viscerally brings you into the present, into the body.

Dance recreates us when we surrender to its flow, when we allow ourselves to be danced, to "sweat our prayers," as Gabrielle Roth says. Dance moves energies like nothing else. Like making love, dance expresses our soul, our pain, our joy, and our resistance, and brings it all, without judgment, into the here and now.

In dance you become a free spirit that can travel into the past, come totally into the present, and see the future. It becomes communion with the Divine: if Shakti is the breath of the Divine, dance is its movement. As both merge, God reveals itself through you.

As dance is the rhythm of the soul, music—the universal language—is its heartbeat. Dance needs music to breathe, move, shift and inspire us to new heights. We are all music, we are all vibration. When the right music comes on, we feel it key into our own vibration, and a chain reaction starts.

Music can create a silent dance within us, one that does not move our bodies externally, yet undulates subtly from within. This silent dance occurs because we constantly generate forms and patterns from sound. It can be said that we are all made up of patterns of sounds that intermingle to create a coherent structure. When sounds come together in this way, music is created.

We all share in this rhythmic intelligence, as rhythmic waves are fluid—easily translated from one octave of vibration to the next. Our senses connect us to these pulsations. In sharing our rhythms with others, we come to a state of communion beyond words, situated in the present moment. This rhythmic communion can be achieved through lovemaking, but it also arises in sound vibration and rhythmic interchange between two or more people.

For example, anthropologist William Condon noted that the Yanamamo tribe in South America synchronize their villages during celebrations and feast days by the exchange of seed syllables between them.

"Each man shouts thirty-two syllables which begin exactly 2/10ths of a second apart. But one man starts exactly 1/10th of a second after the other man. The next burst begins exactly after the stress peak of the second man's third syllable. The result sounds like an angry shouting match, but in fact represents a highly synchronized sound dance—a precise and phase-locked interaction."[*]

This sound dance synchronizes the brain waves of the two men. The effect would be heightened if they marched together, or entrained their breathing and heartbeat patterns to each other. The more you move in rhythm with someone, the more you become like them. Even the audience, the listeners themselves, become entrained to the speakers' speech.

Our bodyminds move in perfect synchrony with the person we are listening to, although we are usually unaware of it. The synchronization deepens if the listener is attentive and involved. Thus the listener does not merely listen and respond—he becomes a part of the speaker, part of the same field. This shows that communication itself is a dance, with everyone involved in intricate and subtle movements across many dimensions.

THE TWO PRIMAL SOUNDS OF SHAKTI

The eighteen pathways open through being activated and charged with breath, light, and sound. Two sounds in particular—*AH* and *OH*—cause the pathways to resonate strongly. When these sounds are sung, all eighteen pathways begin to pulse in unison, vibrating your whole bodymind and soul together as one flow, one pathway, one beingness.

---

[*]William Condon, "Cultural Microrhythms" in M. Davis, ed., *Interaction Rhythms* (New York, Human Sciences Press, 1982).

AH—Opening to Creation

AH is the first sound of creation.
AH opens, creates bliss, manifests life. AH bubbles up joy.
AH releases, heals, and relaxes.
AH unwinds, unfolds, and runs through all of creation:
    every emotion and feeling we have has AH flowing
    through it, if we choose to tune into it.
AH is the sound of the present moment, being here, and
    now.

In any situation, *AH* can be sounded to connect with the essence of any feeling, thought, or idea. It is the first creative force, flowing through our bodies, minds, souls, and world. Whenever we are stuck, confused, angry, or stressed, *AH* is the antidote. It helps us to relax, release, and connect with the essence we may have temporarily forgotten.

AH is an orgasmic sound, one of the main sounds we make when we make love. Making love brings us to our essence, to merging with another and with all life in joy. In making love we forget who we think we are, and simply become present in *AH*.

AH is the blueprint of relationship, and where all relationships meet—in the open, free expression of who you are in all your love, power, and joy, without barrier, inhibition, or restriction. *AH* is where the human and the Divine first form as a divine idea.

AH is the sound of God expressing herself in the first breath of creation, the first note of life, the opening of the Way for light to reveal.

OH—Opening the Womb

OH is the sound that gives life to connection and relationship. It breathes life force into the web of life, energizing and expanding. In its constant unbroken movement, *OH* constantly renews itself in each moment.

OH is the sound of the original womb, the sound that occurs with birth. It is one of the main sounds of orgasm—"Oh, oh, oh!"—when a woman is being penetrated and she truly feels her womb; this is the sound that naturally arises in all women regardless of race or country. *OH* dominates words meaning either the whole or void, such as *womb, dome, hole,* and *moon.* It resonates deep in the belly, opening and softening the womb, connecting it to its primordial clear essence, rich, deep, and whole within itself.

In Sanskrit, *OH* is an aspect of the Moon Goddess Priti, goddess of love, grace, and favor, and of Vijaya—the successful accomplishment of all objectives in life.

BEFORE AND AFTER
THE SHAKTI CIRCUIT

What was once unplugged, disconnected, forgotten has now returned to wholeness. In reflection of myself before the awakening to Shakti, I sense suffering, isolation, numbness, separation. I tune in now and am amazed at the dance that has taken place within my soul; one that now will never cease to be danced.

To feel the flow of light moving on its own, breathing on its own throughout my being is a precious gift to behold. In just sitting quietly now, everything feels different. The eighteen points of the pathway feel electric when I tune into them, whereas before they were just simply parts of the body. The flow between them all is regenerating a charged current through my field . . . makes the body feel viscerally different, more alive even in stillness. (C.O.)

When I tune into the seven gates from the yoni to the deep inner spaces of the womb, I realize what a deep healing has taken place. There is a pregnant emptiness there, like it is ready to create, because the slate is now clean. There is also a deep peace, not just within the gates, but also within all the cells of the body; an invigorated peace, a vibrant stillness unlike any I have known or reached in years of meditation. Earth herself feels different somehow as well, as though her gates have been healed, cleared, and activated along with the collective.

Before the experience, in tuning into the first three gates, and asking what they needed, I was told that the yoni wanted to be sung to, the G-spot to have the floodgates released of the torrent being held back, and the clitoris to be appreciated. Through the exercises and focused intent, these have all been given in abundance and so to tune in with them now, they feel the praise, gratitude, and compassion they should as part of the Divine Woman. It feels as if the entire meaning of being a "woman" has been redefined to its original intent. (T.A.)

There has always been a hesitancy, a holding back, keeping the fires controlled, living in the comfort zone of nurturing, supporting, giving to, and loving others, unaware of the selfishness, that dwelled within that zone, that served the need to be loved, needed, and validated. Honoring the light of our being and skirting or turning away from the darkness is what we were taught.

There have been no teachings shared to take us into the vast realms of the Black Light, until now. There was no understanding of the power within the womb that remained hidden behind the iron doors, both created from within, and through the patriarchy into the collective consciousness of humanity.

Activating the Shakti Circuit with its seven gates, opening to the eighteen point constellation within this female body/mind/world, has triggered memories, healed ancient wounds, stirred the fires of the "sleeping beauties" of passion and creativity and fueled the clarion call to serve in unconditional love for the benefit of all. Diligence, commitment, and dedication in practice will fine-tune the activation and use of this divine flow of both the light and dark rivers of life force intertwined in sacred marriage within.

Forgiveness is a key in these awakening practices, as it is the softening of all rigidity, the letting go of any judgment, preference, projection, or expectation. It is becoming self-responsible for all that you experience. It is the compassionate, humble Presence that allows the flow of Shakti to action in loving service through you. (C.O.)

There is a softness that has imbued my being more totally and more profoundly than I have ever experienced. Women, in our historical and genetic patterns, and related to all of our past incarnations, tend to emerge based either on the side of power or on the side of love. Whichever the case, to move into our truth and balance, it is the opposite that we have to find within ourselves again.

My roots were in power. I was comfortable there in the dark river, unafraid to jump boldly, to strike fiercely, to stand alone . . . and yet there was no compassion in my soul. Very rarely did I sense true, deep emotions running through me. I didn't feel cold or heartless . . . in fact, surface emotions came readily; I often cried at Hallmark commercials, I was touched by mundane moments of humanity and loved on some level.

And yet, moving into the compassionate womb and the light river, I have found a wellspring of peace deep within that allows me to soften and see in a totally different way. It is a peace that imbues empathy and acceptance; a beautiful softness that makes me feel truly feminine as I never have before; and grateful in a new way for everything in and around me. It has stirred within me an understanding of the deeper levels of compassion and Love that we are capable of as true reflections of God in human form. (T.A.)

The Voice of Shakti

I Am the paradox, the juxtaposition of the two most powerful forces of duality. I am at once the river of light, the wellspring from Source that fills, rejuvenates, uplifts, renders blissful, feeds the soul, and can be shared through compassion with all Beings, and the river of darkness, the subtle, hidden realms that few dare enter because the waters hold power, magic, the unknown that the mind is too terrified to even imagine.

Both require total Presence, total surrender, and total commitment to access because once the body flows with me, I cannot be put back to sleep, to lie dormant and forgotten once again. The cells recognize me and call to me to keep flowing to them. So the Soul who comes to me and calls my name needs to be totally committed to the journey they are embarking upon, for they won't be able to turn back.

Some may be lost for a while, only experiencing the light-ness of my being, not even aware as they flew past the early gates, trying to reach the depths where the greatest secrets, the greatest truths must be stored, that they missed something on the journey. This is how humanity is trained—to cross the finish line and reap the reward. Go straight for the seventh gate, the magic God number of seven must be where that which we seek lies. And indeed they will find great things there . . . great tools to heal, transform, transmute, and assist humanity.

Their hearts will deepen into compassion and service by these experiences, for they will be constantly filled with these vibrations of God. And yet, they will miss out on the entirety of God. For those that truly surrender the mind and stay present with me, I will send subtle clues, hints to explore and experience all of me. As any human knows, every being wants to be embraced in their totality. I am no different.

When they explore, they will get a sensing of a deeper, gurgling current that feels very different to what they have experienced of me thus far. If they are persistent, they will find an access point within the second gate where one can dive into the deep well of my darkness. I hold their memories in my depths of the horrors they have lived, inflicted, and avoided seeing because they hold a belief framed with shame and guilt that these weren't also an experience of God. By being willing to surrender to me, they can move through these veils with expedience and be free. All emotions are sacred.

My gift is freedom, freedom from the constraints of even the belief that light and dark exist separately. How can they exist separately when they intertwine and flow together in tandem through the body? When you are totally committed, totally surrendered, totally present to experiencing anything, then you will be free.

Resources

Shakti Circuit Healings and Retreats

THE SHAKTI CIRCUIT CAN BE put into practical application through healings and retreats. For more information visit the author's website:

www.padmaaon.com

To access Shakti Circuit healings, click on the **Healing** link.
To access Shakti Circuit retreats, click on the **Events** link.

ABOUT THE HEALINGS

Some of the specific healings available on the author's website—such as the placenta healing and the atlas adjustment—are mentioned in this book. Several other healings relating to the Shakti Circuit are also described on the website, including a healing for the amygdala and a womb/hara lock. Thousands of people have already received these healings, and their lives have shifted as a result. You can access all of these healings and more on the website. We would love to hear from you.

For more information about receiving an atlas adjustment, you can also go directly to the following website:

www.atlasprofilax.ch

ABOUT THE RETREATS

The Shakti Circuit retreats are powerful and direct experiences. The feminine is now holding and providing the platform for experiences of Christ Consciousness to be integrated and anchored deeply and permanently into the body and mind through timeless and enlightening practices from the Egyptian, Aramaic, Hebrew, and Tantric traditions of the East. These lineages hold the resonance and space for the retreats, and guide retreat participants as an active presence.

Once you experience a Shakti Circuit retreat, you will understand in your very cells and DNA what Shakti is. The resonance and loving power of these retreats can open you to your essence and connection to the Galactic Center, the womb and heart of this galaxy. They are not intellectual teachings, as the core purpose of Shakti is to bring people into their direct knowing. They are deeply transformative. If you are committed, miracles can happen in these retreats. The Shakti Circuit retreats are a co-creation, as each retreat differs according to the consciousness of the group present. Each group co-creates their own retreat according to their highest potential, and their deepest needs.

We welcome and honor you, and look forward to spending more time with you.

Namastute.

Acknowledgments

I THANK Carol Mara, Tanaa Anra, Laura Re, Tarananda, and Whitney for being some of the first people to step through some of the eighteen pathways. Your courage, dedication, commitment, and selfless, total giving are examples of what all need to embody. Much of the writing came through these women as they burned through the fires and activated their eighteen pathways, particularly Tanaa and Carol. The direct voice of Shakti came through to provide some of the experiential revelation that the eighteen pathways contain.

I thank Laura Re for helping me edit the manuscript, and my daughter Isha Prakasha for paving the way for these teachings and revelations to anchor once more on Earth. I love you. Thank you to Whitney for immersing in this more with me, and providing your home for me to complete the writing of this book. Thank you to my Beloved Anaiya for being with me with all of this. I would like to thank also all the priestesses who are now recongregating to bring the Black Light and the loving power of Divine Woman back onto Earth again.

Thank you to Ja-lene Clark, my literary agent, for being a loving support for my work.

Thank you to Jon Graham at Inner Traditions for being open and feeling directly what Shakti is all about.

Thank YOU dear reader for being here on Earth now and stepping forward. I am here to serve you.

Index

232

BOOKS OF RELATED INTEREST

Womb Wisdom
Awakening the Creative and Forgotten Powers of the Feminine
by Padma Aon Prakasha and Anaiya Aon Prakasha

Sacred Relationships
The Practice of Intimate Erotic Love
by Anaiya Sophia and Padma Aon Prakasha

Sacred Sexual Union
The Alchemy of Love, Power, and Wisdom
by Anaiya Sophia

Advanced Spiritual Intimacy
The Yoga of Deep Tantric Sensuality
by Stuart Sovatsky, Ph.D.

Sex, Love, and Dharma
Ancient Wisdom for Modern Relationships
by Simon Chokoisky

Shakti
Realm of the Divine Mother
by Vanamali

The Healing Power of the Sacred Woman
Health, Creativity, and Fertility for the Soul
by Christine R. Page, M.D.

The Path of the Priestess
A Guidebook for Awakening the Divine Feminine
by Sharron Rose

Inner Traditions • Bear & Company
P.O. Box 388
Rochester, VT 05767
1-800-246-8648
www.InnerTraditions.com

Or contact your local bookseller